INDIAN WILLS, 1911 - 1921
Records of the Bureau of Indian Affairs

Book One

INDIAN WILLS, 1911 - 1921
Records of the Bureau of Indian Affairs

Book One

Jeff Bowen

CLEARFIELD

Printed for
Clearfield Company, Inc. by
Genealogical Publishing Co., Inc.
Baltimore, Maryland
2005

International Standard Book Number: 0-8063-5262-0

Made in the United States of America

Introduction

These documents were found in the *Guide to Records in the National Archives of the United States Relating to AMERICAN INDIANS* on page 98, "eight volumes of copies of Indian wills, 1911-21, that, pursuant to the act of 1910 and an act of February 13, 1913 (37 Stat. 678), were referred to the Bureau and the Office of the Secretary of the Interior for Approval."

The Native American wills and probate records were listed under "RECORDS OF THE LAW AND PROBATE DIVISIONS." The Law and Probate Divisions evolved from the Land Division that handled legal matters until a separate law office was established in 1907. By 1911, this office was mostly called the Law Division. An act of June 25, 1910 (36 Stat. 855), authorized by the Secretary of the Interior, was to determine the heirs of deceased Indian trust allottees; both the Land Division and the Law Division handled work resulting from this legislation. In 1913, an Heirship Section was established in the land Division that later was mostly concerned with probate work. By 1917, the Division was usually called the Probate Division.

The wills themselves were never filmed until they were discovered by the author and filmed in 1996. The wills and probate records consisted of 2568 pages.

The wills are not numbered in any certain order; there are 179 pages of wills without index in this volume, consisting of 96 different wills. The majority of the wills are of western origin and a few eastern ones that will be reproduced as more volumes are completed.

In *Book One* alone there are three wills that were actually taken to the highest office in the land, the President of the United States. Two were signed and approved by President Woodrow Wilson and one by President Warren G. Harding.

Some of the tribes included among the wills are Chippewa, Sioux, Apache, Shawnee, Quapaw, Assiniboin, Leach Lake Chippewa, Confederated Flathead, Ponca, Cheyenne, Crow, Sac & Fox, Nez Perce, Southern Ute, Omaha, Osage, and many more.

Jeff Bowen
Hixson, TN

<u>LOUIS PAMBRUM BURDEAU</u>

To whom it may concern know that I, Louis Pambrum Burdeau, being of sound mind do make this my last will and Testament.

Firstly.   I desire that my just indebtedness be paid.

Secondly.   I give and bequeath to my wife, Annie Pambrum Burdeau, all my interest in all the fixtures, household goods, furniture and chattels belonging to my household, all my interest therein all the improvements, houses, fences, stables buildings, wagons of every description, ? mowing ? rakes and all improvements of whatsoever kind I have interest in or own individually or may die personal of to be given to my wife Annie to have and to hold for her individual use and benefit her heirs and assigns forever.

Thirdly.   I give and bequeath unto my wife Annie, all the live stock, horses and cattle that I own or any interest therein or individually.   Also any chattel property or stock of any kind whatever that I may die possessed of and not particulary(sic) mentioned.

Fourthly.   I also give and bequeath unto my wife all and singular full title to one bay horse branded S left shoulder and ? which horse I obtained from Mr. George Save of Seatle Bout Alberto, Canada, in 1898.   I also wish and state that I give to my son, David P Burdeau and to my cousin, James Pambrum Gallineau, the sum of one dollar each.   The aforesaid, David Burdeau and James Gallineau having received from me heretofore their share of my of my(sic) property that I felt disposed to give them.   And I wish to adminisrtatrix to particularly see this last wish administered accordingly.

Fifthly.   I give and bequeath unto my wife Annie and to my children, Isabell, Dora, Thomas, and George Pambrum Burdeau and unto my two grandchildren, Eddie and Annie Pambrum Burdeau any and all real estate or allotment of land allowed to me by the United States Government to be given to them equally. Share and share alike and any other real estate I may inherit or may die possessed of to be given them, their heirs and assignments.

Sixthly.   I also and do now appoint my wife Annie to be the administratrix of this my last will and testament and executor there of and the United States Superintendent.   S Dagt? Indian Agent also.   Each or either of these not to be required to give land in any sum whatever for the fulfilmint(sic) of this appointment.

In witness where of I have hereunto set my hand and seal this Twentith(sic) day of February, 1911.

Louis E Pambrum Barod

Witnesses
John G Galbreath
J B Monroe
Robt. J Hamilton

Personally appeared before me, a Notary Public, in and for the State of Montana, Louis Pambrum Burdeau, to me personally known to be the person whose name is subscribed to the foregoing instrument of writing and acknowledged the same to be his signature and for the uses and purposes therein expressed and to be of his own free will.

James M Amonx

Probate
74941-19
 V L D
DEPARTMENT OF THE INTERIOR
Office of Indian Affairs   SEP 10 1920

The within Will of LOUIS BURDEAU, otherwise known as LOUIS E. PAMBRUM BORAD, is here-by recommended for approval in accordance with the Act of June 25, 1910 (36 Stat. L. 855-6), and the Act of February 14, 1913 (37 Stat. L. 678)

E B Meritt
Assistant Commissioner.

DEPARTMENT OF THE INTERIOR
Office of the Secretary   SEP 10 1920

The within Will is hereby approved in accordance with the provisions of the Act of June 25, 1910 (36 Stat. L. 855-6), and the Act of February 14, 1913 (37 Stat. L. 678).

S G Hopkins
Assistant Secretary

▲▼▲▼▲▼▲▼▲▼▲▼▲▼▲▼

<u>AAGH-NUM-ME</u>

KNOW ALL MEN BY THESE PRESENTS:

That I, Aagh-num-me, a resident of Jackson County, Kansas, being of sound mind and memory, do hereby make, publish and declare this to be my last will and testament, hereby revoking all other and former wills by me at any time made.

ITEM 1.   I desire and direct that before any disposition is made of my property, that all of my just debts including my funeral expenses and the expense of my last illness be paid from the proceeds of any property owned by me at the time of my death.

ITEM 2.   I give, devise and bequeath to my two grandchildren, Shough-na-gish-go-quah and Henrietta Wah-sash-kuck an equal interest in all my rights title and interest in and to allotment #392, described as the SE/4 of the NE/4 of Section 6, Township 9, South of Range 15, East, and the SW/4 of the NW/4 and the N/2 of the SW/4 of Sec. 1, Twp. 9, South of Range 14, East of the 6th P.M., in Kansas, containing 160 acres, and any other property which may subsequently come to me thru inheritance.

It is understood, however, that my right to dispose of said property is not absolute, but is restricted by certain laws, rules and regulations imposed upon me by the Government of the U.S., which restrictions will be removed at the end of a period of time fixed by the United States Government.

ITEM 3.   It is my wish and will that the parties to whom I have bequeathed the above described land, each and both of them, shall be restricted in this, that they shall not have the right to sell, mortgage or otherwise encumber said land during their lifetime, but that same shall pass, at their death, to their legal heirs unencumbered.

IN WITNESS WHEREOF, I have hereunto set my hand this *31st* day of *May* 1917.

Aagh-num-me his mark

We, and each of us, do hereby certify that we saw Aagh-num-me sign his name to the foregoing will and heard him declare that it was his last will and testament, and we, in his presence and in the presence of each other, and at his request, sign the same as witnesses thereto.

IN WITNESS WHEREOF, we have hereunto set our hands this *31ˢᵗ* day of *May* 1917.

J S Bommin, Supt.	*Paul Cadue*
Kickapoo School	*P.O. Route 2, Whiting, Kans*
Germantown, Kans.	*Grant Wewenes?*
	P.O. Route 2, Whiting Kans

DEPARTMENT OF THE INTERIOR
Office of Indian Affairs   SEP 9 1917

The within will of AAGH-NUM-ME deceased Potawatomi allottee No. 392, is here-by recommended for approval in accordance with the Act of June 25, 1910 (36 Stat. L. 855-6), and the Act of February 14, 1913 (37 Stat. L. 678)

E B Meritt
Assistant Commissioner.

DEPARTMENT OF THE INTERIOR
Office of the Secretary   SEP 10 1920

The within will of AAGH-NUM-ME deceased Potawatomi allottee No. 392, is hereby approved in accordance with the provisions of the Act of June 25, 1910 (36 Stat. L. 855-6), and the Act of February 14, 1913 (37 Stat. L. 678).

S G Hopkins
Assistant Secretary

▲▼▲▼▲▼▲▼▲▼▲▼▲▼▲▼

BLANCHE HAAG (WATAN)

LAST WILL AND TESTAMENT OF BLANCHE HAAG (WATAN)

I, Blanche Haag (Watan), wife of Frank (Clarence) Haag of Colony, Oklahoma, being of sound and disposing mind and memory, and understanding, do hereby make, publish and declare the following to be my last will and testament, hereby revoking and annulling all wills and codicils heretofore by me made.

Indian Wills, 1911 – 1921 Book 1
Records of The Bureau of Indian Affairs

FIRST: I direct that my daughter Katherine remain with my mother Baani or Big Face during the remainder of her natural life, thus providing her with a home which I desire that my daughter Katherine be given. I further desire that my daughter Katherine be given a Christian education and that every effort possible be made to provide her with such training as will make of her a Christian young lady.

SECOND: I give, devise, and bequeath to my daughter Katherine, forty acres of my allotment described as the Southwest Quarter of the Northeast Quarter of Section twelve, Township Nine, Range Sixteen, West of the Indian meridian in Washita County, State of Oklahoma, the same to be hers and hers solely during her natural life time. I furthermore give, devise, and bequeath to my beloved husband, Frank (Clarence) Haag, the Southeast quarter of the Northeast Quarter, Section Twelve, Township Nine, Range Sixteen, West of the Indian Meridian in Washita County, State of Oklahoma, same to be his for the remainder of his natural life time. All of the afore-described Real Estate being in Washita County, State of Oklahoma, the tract bequeathed to my daughter Katherine comprising forty acres and the tract bequeathed to my beloved husband, Frank (Clarence) Haag, the remainder forty acres.

THIRD: I give, devise and bequeath to my beloved husband, Frank (Clarence) Haag, one grey horse which is now my property and I further give, devise and bequeath to my beloved father Watan, one buckskin horse which is also my property.

FOURTH: All other property, both real and personal of which I may be possessed at the date of my death, I give, devise and bequeath as follows: One-half to my beloved daughter Katherine and one-half to my beloved husband Frank (Clarence) Haag.

IN TESTIMONY WHEREOF, I have hereunto set my hand and seal at Colony, in the County of Washita, State of Oklahoma, this sixth day of October, nineteen hundred seventeen.

Blanche Haag (Watan)

WITNESSES:
Rilla M Meek Colony, Okla.
Ramon R Youngblood Colony, Okla.

Signed, published and declared by Blanche Haag (Watan) the above named testator, as and for her last will and testament in our presence who, at her request and in her presence and in the presence of each other, have hereunto subscribed our names as attesting witnesses.

Rilla M Meek, Colony, Okla.
Ramon R Youngblood, Colony, Okla.

Subscribed and sworn to before me, Notary Public for and in the State of Oklahoma this 6th day of October 1917.

George Bent
Notary Public

My Commission expires August 29, 1921.

DEPARTMENT OF THE INTERIOR
Office of Indian Affairs   SEP 23 1920

It is hereby recommended that the within will of Blanche Haag (Watan), deceased unallotted Arapaho Indian of the Seger Agency, Oklahoma, be approved in accordance with the provisions of the Act of June 25, 1910 (36 Stat. L. 855-6), and the Act of February 14, 1913 (37 Stat. L. 678), and the Regulations of the Department.

Respectfully
E B Meritt
Assistant Commissioner.

9-MH-22

DEPARTMENT OF THE INTERIOR
Office of the Secretary   SEP 24 1920

The within will of Blanche Haag (Watan), deceased unallotted Arapaho Indian of the Seger Agency, Oklahoma, is hereby approved in accordance with the provisions of the Act of June 25, 1910 (36 Stat. L. 855-6), and the Act of February 14, 1913 (37 Stat. L. 678), and the Regulations of the Department.

S G Hopkins
Assistant Secretary

▲▼▲▼▲▼▲▼▲▼▲▼▲▼

MRS. JOSEPHINE WHITESELL

LAST WILL AND TESTAMENT
OF
Mrs. Josephine Whitesell

Indian Wills, 1911 – 1921 Book 1
Records of The Bureau of Indian Affairs

IN THE NAME OF GOD. AMEN.

I, *Josephine Whitesell* of *Wakupala*(sic), *SD* being of sound mind, memory and understanding, do hereby make and publish this my last will and testament, hereby revoking and annulling all wills by me heretofore made, in manner and form following, that is to say.

First: I direct that all my just debts and funeral expenses, and expenses of my last illness shall be paid by my executor hereinafter named as soon after my decease as convenient;

Second: I give, devise and bequeath to *My husband Smells The Bear the quarter section on which stands my home erects with his described as SE-20-21-28. To my son Charlie, the NE 20-21-28 and my son John SE 17-21-28. To my grandchildren, Elizabeth – Ervin – William – Deihl and Aloina one horse each.*

Third: All the rest and residue of my estate, both real, and personal and mixed, I give, devise and bequeath to my lawful heirs as determined after my decease.

And, I do hereby nominate, constitute and appoint (no name given) executor of this my last will and testament.

In Testimony Whereof, I have set my hand and seal to this, my last will and testament, at *Fort Yates, ND,* this *18* day of *March* in the year of our Lord one thousand, nine hundred and *20*

And lastly, I hereby request *James B Kitt* to sign my name to this my last will and testament and witness the same.

> *Her Mark*
> *Josephine Whitesell*
> (Testator or Testratrix)

Signed, sealed, published and declared by said *Josephine Whitesell* in our presence, as and for *her* last will and testament; and at *her* request and in our presence, and in the presence of each other, we have hereunto subscribed our names as attesting witnesses thereto.

> *James B Kitt* of *Ft Yates ND*
> *Nellie Schoenhut* of *Ft Yates ND*

DEPARTMENT OF THE INTERIOR
Office of Indian Affairs   SEP 23 1920

It is recommended that the within will of Mrs. Josephine Whitesell, deceased Standing Rock Sioux Allottee No. 555, be approved under the Act of June 25, 1910 (36 Stat. L. 855-6), as modified by the Act of February 14, 1913 (37 Stat. L. 678.

> Respectfully
> *E B Meritt*
> Assistant Commissioner.

DEPARTMENT OF THE INTERIOR
Office of the Secretary   SEP 24 1920

The within will is hereby approved under the Act of June 25, 1910 (36 Stat. L. 855-6), as modified by the Act of February 14, 1913 (37 Stat. L. 678).

> Respectfully
> *S G Hopkins*
> Assistant Secretary

▲▼▲▼▲▼▲▼▲▼▲▼▲▼▲▼

RATTLESNAKE DEN

Last Will and Testament of Rattlesnake Den, Fort Peck Indian Allottee No. 1871.

In the name of God, Amen:- , Rattlesnake Den, Fort Peck Indian Allottee No. 1871, sixty seven years of age, being of sound and disposing mind and memory, and not acting under duress, menace, fraud or undue influence of any person whatsoever, do make, publish and declare this my last will and testament, to-wit:-

First. I direct that my body be decently buried.

Second. I hereby will and bequeath unto my husband, Red Horse, otherwise known as Gray Face, who belongs on the Fort Belknap Indian Reservation, one half of my allotment of grazing land, to-wit:- the north-east quarter of Section thirty-six, Township twenty-nine, North, Range forty-three East, M.P.M., containing one hundred sixty acres of land.

Third:- I hereby will and bequeath unto my half-sister, Comes-out Fighter, Fort Peck Indian Allottee No. 1308, the other half of my allotment of grazing land, to-wit:- the north-west quarter of Section thirty-six, Township twenty-nine, North, Range forty-three East, M.P.M., containing one hundred sixty acres of land.

Fourth:- I hereby will and bequeath unto Jack Fighter, Fort Peck Indian Allottee No. 1309, my allotment of irrigable land, to-wit:- the north-east quarter of the south-east quarter of Section thirty-six, Township twenty-seven, North, Range forty-five, East, M.P.M. and also my allotment of timber land, to-wit:- the East half of the North-west quarter of the North-west quarter of Section twelve, Township twenty-six, North, Range forty-five, East, M.P.M.

Fourth(sic); The balance of my real property of which I may be siezed at the time of my death, whether obtained by allotment, purchase, inheritance or otherwise, I will and bequeath to Jack Fighter, Fort Peck Indian Allottee No. 1309.

Fifth. I will and bequeath to my husband, Red Horse, or Gray Face, all the personal property of which I may be siezed at the time of my death.

In witness whereof I have hereunto set my hand and seal this eighth day of January, 1915.

Witnesses to Mark.   her thumb
                                    Rattlesnake Den.
Isaac Miller   mark
Chas E Roblier

The foregoing instrument, consisting of one page, was at the date hereof, by the said Rattlesnake Den, signed, sealed and published as and declared to be her last will and testament; and we, at her request and in her presence, and in the presence of each other, have subscribed our names as witnesses thereto.

Isaac Miller
Chas E Roblier

I, the undersigned, over the age of twenty one years, hereby certify, on honor, that I was present and acted as Interpreter when Rattlesnake Den signed and executed the within instrument and declared it to be her last will and testament; that said instrument was read to and interpreted by me to the said

Rattlesnake Den; and that she thoroughly understood the contents and meaning of the said instrument before she signed it.

Isaac Miller

66364-20
M H W
Approval of Modified Will, Rattlesnake Den, Fort Peck, Mont.

DEPARTMENT OF THE INTERIOR
Office of Indian Affairs   SEP 22 1920

It is recommended that the within will of Rattlesnake Den, deceased Assiniboni allottee No. 1871 of the Fort Peck Reservation be modified in accordance with the intention of the testatrix, and that Makes Cloud be entitled to the land inadvertently devised to Comes Out Fighter, and that the same be approved in accordance with the Act of June 25, 1910 (36 Stat. L. 855-6), as amended by the Act of February 14, 1913 (37 Stat. L. 678.

Respectfully
E B Meritt
Assistant Commissioner.

DEPARTMENT OF THE INTERIOR
Office of the Secretary   SEP 24 1920

Pursuant to the provisions of the Act of June 25, 1910 (36 Stat. L. 855-6), as amended by the Act of February 14, 1913 (37 Stat. L. 678), the within will of Rattlesnake Den, deceased Assiniboini allottee No. 1871 of the Fort Peck Reservation, is hereby approved as modified.

Respectfully
S G Hopkins
Assistant Secretary

GOES HOWLING

OFFICE OF INDIAN AFFAIRS
RECEIVED
IAN 9 -1920

DEPARTMENT OF THE INTERIOR
UNITED STATES INDIAN SERVICE

Indian Wills, 1911 – 1921 Book 1
Records of The Bureau of Indian Affairs

I, Goes Howling, Sioux-Sisseton Indian of the Ft Peck Reservation, being of sound and disposing mind declare this my last will and testament and that at my death there shall be given to Mrs. Halfred Walking Cloud the timber dam, to Elizabeth (Lambert) Drum, Midas Lambert and Wilfred Lambert, the 40 A ittigable land; And the money from the sale of her land (sold last fall) i.e. whatever is left after I die, shall be divided equally among my sons Half red and Eagle Ear (Deafy or No Ear) and to my adopted daughter Lydia Bruguier.

Signed and delivered this day at Drew, Mont. by me.

Her

Goes *Howling*

thumb

In presence of
D.A. Heibert, Teacher DS No. 1
Culbertson, Mont.
Wilbert Love Him (Interpreter)

Probate
2077-20
 V L D

DEPARTMENT OF THE INTERIOR
Office of Indian Affairs   SEP 18 1920

The within Will of GOES HOWLING is hereby recommended for approval according to the provisions of the Act of June 25, 1910 (36 Stat. L. 855-6), as amended by the Act of February 14, 1913 (37 Stat. L. 678).

E B Meritt
Assistant Commissioner.

DEPARTMENT OF THE INTERIOR
Office of the Secretary   SEP 22 1920

The within Will is hereby approved in accordance with the provisions of the Act of June 25, 1910 (36 Stat. L. 855-6), as amended by the Act of February 14, 1913 (37 Stat. L. 678).

S G Hopkins
Assistant Secretary

▲▼▲▼▲▼▲▼▲▼▲▼▲▼

<u>ANNIE FOOTE (ANNA B TAYLOR)</u>

State of Montana)
            (SS   In re. estate of
County of Sheridan)   Annie Foote # 936.

    I, the undersigned, F. E. Farrell, formerly farmer in charge of the Box Elder Sub-station, Brockton, Montana, but now teacher at Day School No. 2, on the Fort Peck Indian Reservation, hereby certify that the following is a copy of a letter written by me to the Supt. of Fort Peck Agency:

    "DEPARTMENT OF THE INTERIOR
"Census.   U.S?Indian Service
                  Brockton, Mont. Nov. 17, 1916.

C.B. Lohmiller, Supt.
Poplar, Mont.

Dear Sir:
    Annie Foots died on Monday, 13th inst. Her family is recorded on the last-late- Census as herself and husband only but they had a baby-girl I think- which is not on the Census. Mrs. Logan Walker has taken the child, as was the desire of the mother and I have written to Mrs. Walker for the name, age, sex and date of birth if known so that it may be properly recorded and also an allotment secured for it.

    I enclose a writing made by her on Sunday which she intended for her Will but which she was too weak to sign and did not regain strength to do so before she died next A. M. This was written by herself in the presence of her mother and sister, Mrs. John Left hand Thunder and Mrs. Bear nose, whose statement I can get if it is of value. As it is confused and they are both interested persons and the paper unsigned I do not think it will go as a valid will tho it was intended for such and her desire is plain.

It reads: "Mr. Roth.
         "xxxxxxxx The baby goes to Mrs. Logan Walker and
         "my land divided to mother, sister and quarter to
         "John Foote Mrs. Walker give adoptage papers to her
         "and about the stack let left hand thunder that at
         "Joes place he has his share out of that hay now
         "so let him have it John Foote never step in the
         "house ever since I was just 2 times but never try to
         "stay this is

Mr. Walker does not want to adopt the baby but will take it in his family to bring up. He paid for the coffin and can be reimbursed from estate and for care of child from its inheritance.

I did not receive request to go and make her will until the day following her death.

When I receive facts of baby's name, etc. willforward.
Respy.
(Sgd.) F. E. Farrell
Farmer in Chg. Dist 1"

The above are the facts as I remember them.
F. E. Farrell
Teacher Day School No. 2

Subscribed and sworn to before me this 20th day of March, 1918.

E. D. Massman
SUPERINTENDENT.

OFFICE OF INDIAN AFFAIRS
RECEIVED
APR 19 1920

Mr Roth

quarter(sic) *to John + divid*(sic)*to my mother, sister + Mrs Walker my land + my baby's land divid that up and pay up my debts and about the timber divid to them too and the baby to Mrs Walker John Foote did not step in the house no more the 21 days I was sick 1 month now. I want made my will for the 5 day May* (NOTE: The above will copied as written, no errors were corrected.)

Statement by Famer(sic) in Charge Dist 1 Fort Peck Agency, Mont.

This document is given me by relatives of Annie Foote, dec Ft Peck Indian, Nov 13, 1916, as being part of her Will and they declare it was written by herself in the presence of the mother, Mrs. Joe Bearnose, her sister, Mrs. John Lefthandthunder, and John Lefthandthunder, a few hours before her death.
FE Farrell
Farmer in Charge Dist 1.
Brockton, Mont. Nov 16-16

Probate
2247-18
V L D   JUL 30 1919

DEPARTMENT OF THE INTERIOR
Office of Indian Affairs

It is recommended that the within will of Anna B Taylor Yanktonai Sioux allottee No. 936, be disapproved under the Act of June 25, 1910 (36 Stat. L. 855-6), as amended by the Act of February 14, 1913 (37 Stat. L. 678).

Respectfully,
C F Hawke
Acting Assistant Commissioner.

DEPARTMENT OF THE INTERIOR
Office of the Secretary   AUG 14 1919

The within will of Anna B Taylor, Yanktonai Sioux allottee No. 936 is hereby disapproved in accordance with the Act of June 25, 1910 (36 Stat. L. 855-6), as amended by the Act of February 14, 1913 (37 Stat. L. 678).

(Signed) S. G. Hopkins
Assistant Secretary

▲▼▲▼▲▼▲▼▲▼▲▼▲▼▲▼

JOHN BARREL

Will John Barrel

I, John Barrel, Ft Peck Indian, Allottee No. 18, resident of Blair, Sheridan Co, Mont, being of sound and disposing mind do make this my last Will and testament, and will my land interests and allotments to my wife Euania, and my children, Mary, aged 9, Marion my daughter aged 8, and Tom my son aged 9 months, to be shared by them according to the state law of Montana.

I give and bequeath at my death to Comes Last, Ft Peck Indian Allottee 179, my red cow and calf, the cow I got from the government, for caring for my family. Signed this 31st day of October, 1916 at Drew, Montana.

Witnesses
F.E. Farrell, Brockton, Mont   *John Barrel* (his thumb print)
Richard Crowe, Brockton, Mont
Interpreter
Richard Crowe

DEPARTMENT OF THE INTERIOR
Office of Indian Affairs   SEP 22 1920

The within will of John Barrell, deceased Yankton Sioux allottee No. 18, of the Fort Peck Reservation, is recommended for approval in accordance with the provisions of the Act of June 25, 1910 (36 Stat. L. 855-6), as amended by the Act of February 14, 1913 (37 Stat. L. 678).

> Respectfully,
> *E B Meritt*
> Assistant Commissioner.

DEPARTMENT OF THE INTERIOR
Office of the Secretary   SEP 24 1920

The within will of John Barrell, deceased Yankton Sioux allottee No. 18 of the Fort Peck Reservation, is hereby approved in accordance with the Act of June 25, 1910 (36 Stat. L. 855-6), as amended by the Act of February 14, 1913 (37 Stat. L. 678).

> *S. G. Hopkins*
> Assistant Secretary

▲▼▲▼▲▼▲▼▲▼▲▼▲▼▲▼

<u>JOHN F CAHILL</u>

IN THE NAME OF GOD, AMEN. Know all men that I, John F. Cahill, Marine Engineer of Newport in the County of Lincoln, State of Oregon, of the age of 60 years, being of sound and disposing mind and memory and not acting under duress, menace, fraud, or undue influence of any person whomsoever, do make, publish, and declare this my last will and testament in manner and form following, to wit:

<u>FIRST</u>: It is my will and I do order that all my just debts and funeral expenses be duly paid and satisfied as soon as conveniently can be done after my decease.

<u>SECOND</u>: I do order and instruct my executor to collect as soon as my be my life insurance amounting to the sum of Two Thousand Dollars and pay over the same to my dear sister (Magdalen) formerly Kate Cahill, a sister of a religious order in the City of Spokane and Sate of Washington, she my said sister Magdalen, otherwise Kate Cahill, out of this said sum of Two Thousand

Dollars to pay all of the funeral expenses and debts of my said estate and outstanding at my decease.

THIRD: I do order and it is my will that the remainder of my estate real and personal be equally divided between my said sister (Magdalen) otherwise Kate Cahill, and my dear sister Cicilia Cahill of the state of Washington, share and share alike, the manner of division to be decided upon by the legatees themselves whether it be a division of the property itself or a sale thereof and division of the money realized by said sale, they themselves to decide and agree upon.

And lastly, I do appoint and constitute John Buckley of Newport, Oregon, the executor, without bonds, of this my last will, hereby revoking all other wills, legacies and bequests by me heretofore made and declaring this and no other to be my last will and testament.

IN WITNESS WHEREOF, I have hereunto set my hand this 2nd day of May A. D. 1912.

Signed   John F. Cahill   (Seal)

The above instrument was on the date thereof signed, sealed published and declared by the said John F. Cahill as and for his last will and testament in the presence of us who at his request and in his presence and in the presence of each other have subscribed our names as witnesses thereto.

John Miller
Edward Pyburn

DEPARTMENT OF THE INTERIOR
Office of Indian Affairs   JUL 23 1920

The within will of John F Cahill deceased white man of Siletz, Oregon, is hereby recommended for approval according to the Act of June 25, 1910 (36 Stat. L. 855-6), as amended by the Act of February 14, 1913 (37 Stat. L. 678), and the Regulations of the Department, but no rights of an executor are recognized.

E B Meritt
Assistant Commissioner.

DEPARTMENT OF THE INTERIOR
Office of the Secretary

Indian Wills, 1911 – 1921 Book 1
Records of The Bureau of Indian Affairs

The within will of John F Cahill deceased white man of Siletz, Oregon, is hereby approved according to the Act of June 25, 1910 (36 Stat. L. 855-6), as amended by the Act of February 14, 1913 (37 Stat. L. 678), and the Regulations of the Department, but no rights of an executor are recognized.

S. G. Hopkins
Assistant Secretary

STATE OF OREGON,)
) SS
County of Lincoln   )

I ....County Clerk and Clerk of the Court of the County and State aforesaid, do hereby certify that the foregoing copy of .... has been compared with the original and that it is a correct transcript therefrom and of the whole of such original.....as the same appears.........at my office and in my custody.

In Testimony Whereof I have hereunto set my hand and affixed the seal of said Court this .... of ....191.....

.... Clerk
.... Deputy

(NOTE: Unable to read any of the above handwriting. Not dark enough.)

▲▼▲▼▲▼▲▼▲▼▲▼▲▼▲▼

CHARLES D STUART

WILL AND TESTAMENT

KNOW ALL MEN BY THESE PRESENTS, That Charles D. Stuart, of Ilwaco, Pacific County, State of Washington, of the age of 51 years and being of sound and disposing mind and memory, and not acting under duress, menace, fraud or the undue influence of any person whatever, do make, publish and declare this my last Will and Testament, in manner following, that is to say:

FIRST.-I desire that my body be decently buried with proper regard to my station and condition in life, and the circumstances of my estate.

SECONDLY.-I direct that my executrix hereinafter named, as soon as she has sufficient funds in her hands, pay my funeral expenses and the expenses of my last sickness, and the allowanees(sic) hereinafter named.

THIRDLY.-I give, devise and bequeath to my beloved wife Rebecca L. Stuart, the sum of One Dollar, and all of Lots No. Eight, (8), Nine, (9), and Ten, (10) in Block No. Fourteen, (14), in Argyle Park Addition to Portland, Multnomah County, State of Oregon, to have and to hold unto her and unto her heirs and assigns forever.

FOURTHLY.-I give, devise and bequeath to my beloved son Ernest Cecil Stuart, all of the rest, residue and remainder of all of my real estate and personal property and effects of every name and nature whatsoever, owned by me at the time of my death, to have and to hold unto him and his heirs and assigns forever. PROVIDED, however, that in case said son who is a minor shall depart this life before he becomes of age, then in that case, I give, devise and bequeath all of the said rest, residue and remainder of my said estate to my wife Rebecca L Stuart to have and to hold unto her, her heirs and assigns forever.

LASTLY.-I hereby nominate and appoint my said wife Rebecca L Stuart, of Ilwaco Pacific County, State of Washington, the executrix of this my last will and testament, hereby revoking all former wills by me made, and I desire and request that she act as such without bonds, and I further desire and request that she be appointed the guardian of my said son.

IN WITNESS WHEREOF I have hereunto set my hand and seal on this the 20th day of January, A.D. 1912.

Chas. D. Stuart SEAL

The foregoing instrument consisting of this page, was, at the date hereof, by the said Charles D Stuart, signed and sealed and published as, and declared by him to be his last will and testament, in the presence of us, who, in his presence and at his request and in the presence of each other have signed our names as witnesses thereunto.

Edward Taft
Residence, Ilwaco, Washington.
C. R. Hart
Residence Ilwaco, Washington.

DEPARTMENT OF THE INTERIOR
Office of Indian Affairs   JUL 8 1920

It is hereby recommended that the within will of Charles D. Stuart, deceased Taholah allottee No. 430 be approved in so far the trust property of the testator is concerned, according to the Act of June 25, 1910 (36 Stat. L. 855-6), as amended by the Act of February 14, 1913 (37 Stat. L. 678), and the Regulations of the Department, but no rights of an executor will be recognized.

Respectfully,
E B Meritt
Assistant Commissioner.

DEPARTMENT OF THE INTERIOR
Office of the Secretary

The within will of Charles D. Stuart, deceased Taholah allottee No. 430, is hereby approved under the provisions of the Act of June 25, 1910 (36 Stat. L. 855-6), as amended by the Act of February 14, 1913 (37 Stat. L. 678), and the Regulations of the Department, but no rights of an executor will be recognized.

S. G. Hopkins
Assistant Secretary

▲▼▲▼▲▼▲▼▲▼▲▼▲▼▲▼

JOHN SHINEWAY

I, John Shineway of the Town of Sand Lake, in the County of Burnett, in the State of Wisconsin, being of sound mind and memory, do make, publish, and declare this my last will and testament, hereby revoking all former wills, bequests and devises by me make:

After all my just debts and funeral expenses have been paid, I do hereby give and bequeath unto my two daughters, all my real and personal property, to share same equally, each an undivided one fourteenth interest in Chippewa Indian Allottee No 19, as determined by the Secretary of the Interior, Feb. 26, 1917. Said Allotment being the SE of SW of Sec. 20 and NE of NW of Sec 29, Tp 39 N.R. 7 W.

The names of my daughters being; Josephine Shineway Taylor and Lida Shineway Taylor.

It is my desire that my daughter Lida Shineway Taylor have the house in which I am now living. Also Lot three (3) in Section twenty seven (27) in

Township thirty-nine (39) North of Range Fifteen (15) West of the Fourth Principal Meridian in Wisconsin.

The above described Lot 3-27-39-15, to be shared equally by the above named daughters.

I do hereby constitute and appoint __(blank)__ execute__(blank)____ of this my last will and testament.

In Witness Whereof, I have hereunto set my hand and seal this 23th(sic) day of April A.D. 1917

his

Witness to signature and to Mark.   John X Shineway. (L.S.)
      Larry Laursen   mark.
      Mrs. Josephine Laursen.

The foregoing instrument was signed, sealed, published and declared by the said John Shineway as and for his last will and testament in the presence of us, who, at his request, in his presence, and in presence of each other, have hereunto subscribed our names attesting witnesses; and said testator was then of sound and disposing mind and memory:

Harry Laursen, Shell Lake, Wis.
Mea. Josephine Laursen, Shell Lake, Wis.

DEPARTMENT OF THE INTERIOR   45120-18
Office of Indian Affairs

I have the honor to recommend that the within certified copy of the original will of John Shineway, deceased unallotted Chippewa Indian of the Lac Courte Creille Reservation, be submitted to the President of the United States for his approval.

E B Meritt
Assistant Commissioner.

DEPARTMENT OF THE INTERIOR
Office of the Secretary   JUL 27 1920

I have the honor to recommend that the within certified copy of the original will of John Shineway, a deceased Chippewa Indian of the Lac Courte Creille Reservation, Wisconsin, be approved, the original will having been duly executed   in   accordance   with   the   laws   of   Wisconsin.

S. G. Hopkins
Assistant Secretary

The White House,
Approved, *29 July* 1920

Woodrow Wilson

▲▼▲▼▲▼▲▼▲▼▲▼▲▼

STONEWALL JACKSON

LAST WILL AND TESTAMENT OF STONEWALL JACKSON

I, Stonewall Jackson, of the County of Ottawa and State of Oklahoma, allottee number sixty six of the Eastern Shawnee Tribe of Indians, seventy-two years of age, being of sound and disposing mind and realizing the certainty of death and uncertainty of the time there, do publish and declare this as my LAST WILL AND TESTAMENT in manner and form as follows:

FIRST: That all my just debts and funeral expenses shall be paid.

SECOND: I give and bequeath to Andrew Dushane, Charles Dushane, David Dushane, Junior, and Daniel Dushane, Lot 1 of section thirty one, the SE/4 of NW/4 and NE/4 of SW/4 of section thirty two and the N/2 of NW/4 of section thirty-three all in township twenty-eight north of range twenty-four east of the Indian Meridian, in Ottawa County, Oklahoma, and all other property both personal mixed and real of which I may die siezed(sic), to share the same equally, share and share alike.

IN WITNESS WHEREOF, I have hereunto set my hand and seal in the said County of Ottawa and State of Oklahoma, on this the fourth day of February, in the year of our Lord One Thousand Nine Hundred and Twenty.

his right

Stonewall Jackson

thumb mark

Signed, sealed, published and declared by Stonewall Jackson, the above named testator, in the presence of us, who at his request in his presence and in t he presence of each other, have hereunto set our names as subscribing and attesting witnesses to the foregoing instrument as the LAST WILL AND TESTAMENT of the said Stonewall Jackson on this the fourth day of February in the year of our Lord One Thousand Nine Hundred and twenty.

Carl F. Mayer	of	*Wyandotte, Oklahoma*
Elliott C Sawtell	of	*Wyandotte, Oklahoma*

DEPARTMENT OF THE INTERIOR
Office of Indian Affairs

It is hereby recommended that the within will of Stonewall Jackson, deceased Quapaw allottee No. 66 be approved in accordance with the provisions of the Act of June 25, 1910 (36 Stat. L. 855-6), as amended by the Act of February 14, 1913 (37 Stat. L. 678), and the Regulations of the Department, but no rights of an executor are to be recognized.

Respectfully,
E B Meritt
Assistant Commissioner.

DEPARTMENT OF THE INTERIOR
Office of the Secretary
SEP 14 1920

The within will of Stonewall Jackson, deceased Quapaw allottee No. 66, is approved in accordance with the provisions of the Act of June 25, 1910 (36 Stat. L. 855-6), as amended by the Act of February 14, 1913 (37 Stat. L. 678), and the Regulations of the Department, but no rights of an executor will be recognized.

S. G. Hopkins
Assistant Secretary

▲▼▲▼▲▼▲▼▲▼▲▼▲▼▲▼

WALKING RED

WILL OF WALKING RED #995 FORT PECK MONT INDIAN.

I, Walking Red, Yankton Indian, Allottee 995 of Fort Peck Resv. Mont. widow, aged 89 years, being of sound mind and wishing to dispose of my property at my death do hereby declare this my last Will and testament and wish that at my death my property shall all be given to Charles Takes Them, Yankton Indian of Fort Peck reservation, Mont, aged 48 years and residing at Brockton, Sheridan County, Mont.

The estate and property I hereby will to him and wish given to him is as follows:

My grazing allotment of 320 acres, described as E 1/2 of Sec 23 of T 28 and R 53,

My 40 acre tract allotment described as NW 1/4 of SW 1/4 of Sec 25, T 28, R 53

My 20 acre timber allotment described as allotment 995 In Sec 1 of T 27, R 53,

These three described allotments being on the Fort Peck Reservation, Sheridan Co, Mont.

My reason for making Charles Takes Them my sole heir to this property is that he has been as my son and cared for me for the past seven years.

I purposely do not will any share in my estate to my distat(sic) relatives, Begs His Own and Beavertail, or any other relative for the reason that Charles Takes Them has been the only one taking care of me for the past seven years and he has been as a son to me and this I have told to the relatives herein mentioned and they know this is my wish as to my property here described.

Signed by me and delivered this date, March 13, 1918, at Box Elder Station, Brockton, Mont.

Interpreted by Maurice Big Horn, of Brockton, Mont.
Witnesses:

Harold Red Eagle   *her*
   Brockton, Mont.
F. E. Farrell, Farmer, I.D.   *thumb*
   Brockton, Mont.

I hereby certify that I prpeared(sic) this Will at the request of Walking Red, who signed this instrument in my presence; that it is according to her wishes; that she was of good mental capacity and strength of body and answered promptly and clearly and properly a series of question(sic) I asked her; that she chatted and laughed in correcting herself and in converse with others; that she appeared very emphatically to dispose of her property and estate as here stated to Charles Takes Them and gave here reasons therefor(sic) and reason for excluding any other persons or relatives from participating in her estate.

F.E. Farrell
Indian Service Farmer
Brockton, Mont. March 13, 1916   *Fort Peck Reservation, Mont.*

DEPARTMENT OF THE INTERIOR
Office of Indian Affairs   AUG 28 1920
(Unable to read this section, print too light)

> Respectfully,
> *E B Meritt*
> Assistant Commissioner.

DEPARTMENT OF THE INTERIOR
Office of the Secretary

(Unable to read this section, print too light)

> *S. G. Hopkins*
> Assistant Secretary

▲▼▲▼▲▼▲▼▲▼▲▼▲▼▲▼

<u>CORA HAMPTON HOLLANDSWORTH</u>

ORIGINAL

OFFICE OF INDIAN AFFAIRS
RECEIVED
JUN 19 1916
66642

   I, Cora Hampton Hollandsworth, of the Eastern Shawnee Tribe of Indians, Quapaw Agency, Oklahoma, Allottee No. 7, of said tribe, being now in good health, strength of body and mind, but sensible of the uncertainty of life, and desiring to make disposition of my property and affairs while in health and strength, do hereby make, publish, and declare the following to be my past(sic) will and testament, hereby revoking and cancelling(sic) all other or former wills by me at any time made.

1. I direct the payment of all my just debts and funeral expenses.

2. I give and devise to my two unallotted minor children the following described portion of my allottment, viz:

To Opal Fay Hollandsworth, the SW/4 of the NE/4 of section 7.

To Ida May Hollandsworth, the NW/4 of the SE/4 of Section 7, all in Township 27, North of Range 25, East of the Indian Meridian in Oklahoma, containing in all, eighty acres, thus providing forty acres for each of these two children.

That any other property possessed by me at my demise, descend in accordance with the law to my legal heirs.

In witness whereof, I, Cora Hampton Hollandsworth have to this, my last will and testament consisting of one sheet of paper, subscribed my name by thumb-mark this 15th day of June, 1916.

Her thumb-mark
Cora Hampton Hollandsworth-

Subscribed by Cora Hampton Hollandsworth, in the presence of each of us, the undersigned, and at the same time declared by her to us to be her last will and testament, and we, thereupon at the request of Cora Hampton Hollandsworth, in her presence and in the presence of, each other, sign our names hereto as witnesses this 15th day of June, 1916.

Witnesses:

> *B.N. O. Walker*
> Wyandotte, Oklahoma
> *C.O. Lennon*
> Wyandotte, Oklahoma
> *John W. Chandler*
> Wyandotte, Oklahoma

DEPARTMENT OF THE INTERIOR
Office of Indian Affairs

It is recommended that the within will be approved in pursuance of the provisions of the Act of June 25, 1910 (36 Stat. L. 855-6), as amended by the Act of February 14, 1913 (37 Stat. L. 678).

Respectfully,
E B Meritt
Assistant Commissioner.

DEPARTMENT OF THE INTERIOR
Office of the Secretary

FEB 24 1917
The within will is hereby approved in pursuance of the provisions of the Act of June 25, 1910 (36 Stat. L. 855-6), as amended by the Act of February 14, 1913 (37 Stat. L. 678).

Bo Sweeney
Assistant Secretary

▲▼▲▼▲▼▲▼▲▼▲▼▲▼▲▼

<u>**UNCLE SAM**</u>

DEPARTMENT OF THE INTERIOR
UNITED STATES INDIAN SERVICE

" WILL "

----

male

IN THE NAME OF GOD: AMEN: I Uncle Sam, an Assiniboin/Indian,of Wolf Point, Montana, born in the year 1835, A.D. and allottee No. 1709; Being of sound mind, but of infirm body, do hereby and by these presents make, declare, and publish this to be my last WILL and Testament.

1st, I hereby give, devise, and bequeath unto Two Eagle, an Assiniboin male Indian of Wolf Point, Montana, born in the year 1880, no relationship, 160 acres of my grazing allotment, described as the NE/4, of Sec. 36, Tp. 30 N, R 45 E; In consideration of the many kindnesses shown me in my old age.

2nd, I hereby direct, that after a decent burial is given me, that all other property of which I may die possessed be distributed to my natural heirs, in accordance with the laws of the state of Montana.

IN WITNESS WHEREOF, I have hereunto set my hand this the *19* day of April, in the year 1916.   His

Uncle Sam   (thumb print)
Mark.

We, the undersigned hereby certify that we were present at, and witnessed the signing by Uncle Sam, of the above WILL, and that *he* signed the same in the presence of each of us, and that it was *his* voluntary act, and that we have signed the WILL as witnesses in the presence of each other, and in the presence of the testator, on the day and year above written.

Victor E Brown
Clinton Fisk
Charles Jackson

DEPARTMENT OF THE INTERIOR
Office of Indian Affairs   OCT 12 1920
The within will of Uncle Sam, deceased Assiniboin allottee No. 1709 of the Fort Peck Reservation, is recommended for approval in accordance with the provisions of the Act of June 25, 1910 (36 Stat. L. 855-6), as amended by the Act of February 14, 1913 (37 Stat. L. 678).

Indian Wills, 1911 – 1921 Book 1
Records of The Bureau of Indian Affairs

Respectfully,
E B Meritt
Assistant Commissioner.

DEPARTMENT OF THE INTERIOR
Office of the Secretary
The within will of Uncle Sam, deceased Assiniboin allottee No. 1709 of the Fort Peck Reservation, is hereby approved in accordance with the provisions of the Act of June 25, 1910 (36 Stat. L. 855-6), as amended by the Act of February 14, 1913 (37 Stat. L. 678).

SG Hopkins
Assistant Secretary

▲▼▲▼▲▼▲▼▲▼▲▼▲▼

SARAH DeFOND McBRIDE

LAST WILL AND TESTAMENT OF SARAH DeFOND McBRIDE

IN THE NAME OF GOD AMEN.

I, Sarah DeFond McBride, of Charles Mix County, South Dakota, being of sound mind and memory, but being uncertain of life and certain of the approach of death, do make and declare this to be my last will and testament, hereby revoking and annulling all other wills heretofore made by me.

First: I give and bequeath to my husband James McBride that portion of my land described as Lot 916 according to the Yankton Survey, located in Charles Mix county, South Dakota; to have and to hold during yhr(sic) remainder of his life, but it is not to be disposed of until his death when it is to descend to his legal heirs.

Second: I give and bequeath unto my son Harry McBride that portion of my land described as Lot 920 according to the Yankton Survey, situated in Charles Mix county South Dakota, to have and to hold during the life of his father, the said James McBride, but it is not to be disposed of while his father lives, but upon the death of his father, James McBride, the title to this land is to become absolute in the said Harry McBride, and may disposed of at his will.

Third: I give and bequeath unto my grand daughter Mary Miner the sum of $100.00, one hundred dollars, from any moneys that I may have to my credit at the time of my death, or that may be derived from the proceeds of any other property belonging to me not previously disposed of.

Fourth: I give and bequeath in equal shares to my husband, James McBride and my son, Harry McBride, all the remainder of my property, of whatsoever nature, both real and personal, of which I may be assessed at the time of my death, after all my just debts and funeral expenses have been paid, and the foregoing provisions of this will have been complied with, and a monument has been erected at my grave to cost $200.

IN TESTIMONY WHEREOF, I have set my hand and seal this *30* day of June, 1919, at my home at Chouteau Creek, Charles Mix County, South Dakota.

Sarah DeFond McBride (her thumb print)

Signed, sealed, published and declared this *30* day of June, 1919, by the said Sarah DeFond McBride, in our presence, as being her last will and testament, and at her request and in her presence, and in the presence of each other, we have hereunto subscribed our names as attesting witnesses.

John McBride, Sr
Dante, S.D.
Maggie Claymore   her (her thumb print)
Dante, S.D.   mark

Probate
9573-20
 M H W   Approval of will

DEPARTMENT OF THE INTERIOR
Office of Indian Affairs   OCT 13 1920

It is hereby recommended that the within will of Sarah DeFond McBride, deceased Yankton Sioux allottee No. 594, be approved under the provisions of the Act of June 25, 1910 (36 Stat. L. 855-6), as amended by the Act of February 14, 1913 (37 Stat. L. 678), and the regulations of the Department.

Respectfully,
E B Meritt
Assistant Commissioner.

DEPARTMENT OF THE INTERIOR
Office of the Secretary   OCT 14 1920

The within will of Sarah DeFond McBride, deceased Yankton Sioux allottee No. 594, is hereby approved in accordance with the provisions of the Act of June 25, 1910 (36 Stat. L. 855-6), as amended by the Act of February 14, 1913 (37 Stat. L. 678), and the regulations of the Department.

SG Hopkins
Assistant Secretary

OFFICE OF INDIAN AFFAIRS
RECEIVED
APR 1 - 1919
28363

AH-ZHOW-E-BIN-AIS

LAST WILL AND TESTAMENT OF AH-ZHOW-E-BIN-AIS.

I, Ah-zhow-e-bin-ais of the Leech Lake Indian Reservation, in Minnesota, being of sound mind and lawful age do hereby make, publish and declare this to be my last will and testament.

FIRST: All of my debts and funeral expenses shall be paid and thereafter I give and bequeath to my sister She-bah-cumig-oke, one-half of all of my estate, real, personal and mixed, of which I may die seised(sic).

SECOND: To my nephew Richard Day, I give and bequeath one-half of all of my estate, real, personal and mixed, of which I may die seised(sic).

THIRD: In the event of the death of either of my heirs under this will, his or her share of the real estate that may still be entact, unsold and the proceeds undivided, same shall descend to my surviving heir.

In witness whereof I have signed, sealed, published and declared this instrument as my last will and testament at Onigum, Minnesota, this 17th day of January, D.D. 1919.

         His right
    Ah zhow e bom ais (thumb print)
         thumb mark

This instrument was on the day of the date thereof signed, published and declared by the said testator to be his last will and testament, in our presence, who, at his request, have subscribed our names thereto as witnesses, in his presence and in the presence of each other.

Indian Wills, 1911 – 1921 Book 1
Records of The Bureau of Indian Affairs

Peter Graves   , Residing at Onigum, Minnesota.
Henry E Bongo   , Residing at Onigum, Minnesota.
Edward Johnson   , Residing at Onigum, Minnesota.

DEPARTMENT OF THE INTERIOR
Office of Indian Affairs OCT -5 1920

It is hereby recommended that the within will of Ah-zhow-e-bin-ais, deceased Leech Lake allottee be approved in accordance with the provisions of the Act of June 25, 1910 (36 Stat. L. 855-6), as amended by the Act of February 14, 1913 (37 Stat. L. 678), and the regulations of the Department.

        Respectfully,
        E B Meritt
        Assistant Commissioner.

DEPARTMENT OF THE INTERIOR
Office of the Secretary OCT 16 1920

The within will of Ah-zhow-e-bin-ais, deceased Leech Lake allottee is hereby approved in accordance with the provisions of the Act of June 25, 1910 (36 Stat. L. 855-6), as amended by the Act of February 14, 1913 (37 Stat. L. 678), and the regulations of the Department.

        SG Hopkins
        Assistant Secretary

▲▼▲▼▲▼▲▼▲▼▲▼
MRS. KNUTE HAGEN (JULIA COBELL)

BLACKFEET AGENCY BROWNING, MONTANA	
RECEIVED	FEB 16 1916
FILE NO.	61119

Bemidji, Minn, May 22nd 1915

I Mrs. Knute Hagen, this twenty second day of May Nineteen hundred and fifteen, wish to will to to(sic) my daughter Traphena, one house and lot in the city of Cut Bank, Montana, one mare, also one third of three hundred and twenty acres on the Cut Bank river, on the Black Foot reservation.

One third of said three hundred and twenty acres of the land to my son Jerald Amund One third to my husband Mr. Knute Hagen. Also to my daughter Traphena, my son Jerald and my husband Knute Hagen. To each of the above named I leave one third of buildings and machinery, etc. on above three hundred twenty acres of land.

I wish Mrs. W.E. Hagerty of Browning, Montana, to have the care of my daughter until she becomes of age and I wish my husband to have the care of my son. Signed   Mrs Knute A Hagen

Witnesses] Elizabeth Penday Gordon Burns F J Danogh

Probate
61119-20
VLD

DEPARTMENT OF THE INTERIOR
Office of Indian Affairs   OCT 15 1920
The within will of Mrs. Knute A. Hagen, otherwise known as Julia Cobell, is hereby recommended for approval in accordance with the Act of June 25, 1910 (36 Stat. L. 855-6), as amended by the Act of February 14, 1913 (37 Stat. L. 678).

> Respectfully,
> *E B Meritt*
> Assistant Commissioner.

DEPARTMENT OF THE INTERIOR
Office of the Secretary
The within will is hereby approved in accordance with the provisions of the Act of June 25, 1910 (36 Stat. L. 855-6), as amended by the Act of February 14, 1913 (37 Stat. L. 678)

> *A T Vogelsang*
> First Assistant Secretary

▲▼▲▼▲▼▲▼▲▼▲▼▲▼▲▼

ALL BLOSSOMS or MRS. BLACK CHEST

LAST WILL AND TESTAMENT

I, All Blossoms, or Mrs. Black Chest, of sound mind and disposing memory, do make, declare and publish this, my last will and testament, hereby revoking and annulling any and all others wills heretofore made by me.

1st.   It is my will and desire that the expense of my last sickness and funeral be paid.

2nd.   That all my just debts be paid.

3rd.   I do hereby will, bequeath, and devise to my adopted daughter, Julia P Grinnell, all my right, title and interest in and to the following described real estate:

The South One-half, (S1/2), of Sect6ion Thirty-four, (34), Township One Hundred Forty-nine, (149), North of Range Ninety-one, (91), and the East One-half of the South-east One quarter, (E1/2SE1/4), of Section Thirty-Three, (33), in Township One Hundred Forty-nine, (149), North of Range Ninety-one, (91), all West of the Fifth, (5th), P.M., in North Dakota, and containing Four Hundred, (400), acres more or less according to the U.S. Govt. Survey thereof.

4th.   I do hereby will, bequeath and devise to Julia P. Grinnell, all other property of which I may die possessed, both real and personal.

5th.   I have no near relatives other than my husband, and he agrees with me in the distribution of my property. It is my desire that no other person or persons than those mentioned shall have any part or portion of my estate.

6th.   I do hereby constitute and appoint Charles F Huber, and Indian of the Fort Berthold Reservation, N Dak., who has been granted citizenship and fee simple patent to his lands, the executor of this my last will and testament and do hereby request that he act as such.

In witness whereof I have hereunto published and declared the foregoing instrument to be my last will and testament, at Elbowoods, N. Dak., on the 22nd day of January, 1918, and have hereunto signed my name as evidence thereof.

Her
All Blossoms   (thumb print)
mark

On the 22nd day of January, 1918, at Elbowoods, N.D.   we the undersigned, were requested to sign the foregoing instrument as witnesses to the will of All Blossoms, or Mrs. Black Chest, by the said All Blossoms, or Mrs. Black Chest, making such request, she at the same time declaring it to be her last will and testament, and publishing the same as such, she signing her name in our presence, and we subscribing thereto in her presence, and in the presence of each other.

Name *Walter Stink Face*	Name *M. H. McKee,*
Age *27*	Age *21*
Residence *Elbowoods, North Dak*	Residence *Elbowoods, N.D.*

Indian Wills, 1911 – 1921 Book 1
Records of The Bureau of Indian Affairs

Probate
83540-20
V L D

DEPARTMENT OF THE INTERIOR
Office of Indian Affairs   OCT 23 1920

It is hereby recommended that the within will of All Blossoms or Mrs. Black Chest, deceased Fort Berthold allottee Nos. 157 and A-855, be approved in accordance with the provisions of the Act of June 25, 1910 (36 Stat. L. 855-6), as amended by the Act of February 14, 1913 (37 Stat. L. 678), and the Regulations of the Department.

> Respectfully,
> *E B Meritt*
> Assistant Commissioner.

DEPARTMENT OF THE INTERIOR
Office of the Secretary   OCT 25 1920

The within will of All Blossoms or Mrs. Black Chest, deceased Fort Berthold allottee Nos. 157 and A-855 is hereby approved in accordance with the provisions of the Act of June 25, 1910 (36 Stat. L. 855-6), as amended by the Act of February 14, 1913 (37 Stat. L. 678), and the Regulations of the Department.

> *Alexander Vogelsang*
> First Assistant Secretary

▲▼▲▼▲▼▲▼▲▼▲▼▲▼▲▼

THERESE CURLY   JAN 10 1920
Flathead Agency,
DIXON, MONTANA   *St. Ignatius, Mont.*
Jan 7 - 1920

The last will and testament of Therese Curly a member of the Confederated Flathead tribe of Indians, being of sound mind deposes and says before these witnesses and in the presence of each other and before God Amen. I hereby bequeath my allotment No. 224 - to my two daughters Christine and Cecile. And my interest in my deceased Lou Stephen Curly's allotment.

I bequeath to Cecile Jillier who I want to have my two girls to care for and keep as her own Cecile and Christine.

Signed this the 7th day of Jan, 1920 in the presence of both of us and in each others presence.

Her
Therese Curly (thumb print)
mark

Witnesses
Norman J Perkins
      St. Ignatius, Mont
N.B. McCoy
      St. Ignatius, Mont.

Probate
48382-20

DEPARTMENT OF THE INTERIOR
Office of Indian Affairs   OCT 21 1920

The within will of Therese Curley, is hereby recommended for approval in accordance with the Act of June 25, 1910 (36 Stat. L. 855-6), as amended by the Act of February 14, 1913 (37 Stat. L. 678).

Respectfully,
E B Meritt
Assistant Commissioner.

DEPARTMENT OF THE INTERIOR
Office of the Secretary   OCT 27 1920
The within will is hereby approved in accordance with the Act of June 25, 1910 (36 Stat. L. 855-6), as amended by the Act of February 14, 1913 (37 Stat. L. 678).

Alexander Vogelsang
First Assistant Secretary

▲▼▲▼▲▼▲▼▲▼▲▼▲▼▲▼

DAVID SITS POOR

𝔚𝔦𝔩𝔩

I, **David Sits Poor** of the Pine Ridge Agency, South Dakota, Allottee number **2817** do hereby make and declare this to be my last will and testament, in accordance with Section 2 of the Act of June 25, 1910, (36 stat. 855-858), and Act of February 14, 1913, (Public No. 381), hereby revoking all former wills made by me:

Indian Wills, 1911 – 1921 Book 1
Records of The Bureau of Indian Affairs

1. I hereby direct that, as soon as possible after my decease, that all my debts, funeral and testamentary expenses be paid out of my personal estate.

2. I give and devise my allotment on the Pine Ridge Reservation, South Dakota, described as follows: **Lots 3 & 4 & S 1/2 of N.W.1/4 of sec 4 in Twp. 39 N of Range 45 West of 6th. Principal Meridian So. Dak.**

in the following manner:
To be given jointly to my Father Sits Poor and my Mother Captured.

3. I give and bequeath all of my personal property of whatsoever nature and wheresoever situated unto **my father and mother.**

4. All the rest of my property, real or personal, now possessed or hereafter acquired, of whatsoever nature and wheresoever situated. I hereby give, devise and bequeath unto **my father and mother.**

In witness whereof I have hereunto set my hand this 16*th* day of *August,* 191*8*

Witness   *Judson Shook*
             Manderson, S.D.   *David Sits Poor*
             Sam Ladiney
             Manderson, S.D.

The above statement was this **16th** day of **August 1918** 191.... signed and published by **David Sits Poor** as **his** last will and testament in the joint presence of the undersigned, the said **David Sits Poor** then being of sound and vigorous mind and free from any constraint or compulsion: whereupon we, being without any interest in the matter other than friendship, and being well acquainted with **him** but not members of **his** family, immediately subscribed our names hereto in the presence of each other and of the said testator, for the purpose of attesting the said will, as (he) requested us to do. And that I **Judson Shook** at the testa**tors** 's request have written **his** name in ink and that **I** affixed **his** thumbmarks.

Post Office Address
Manderson S. D.
Manderson So. Dak.

Pine Ridge, South Dakota.
October 8, 1920.

I hereby certify that I have fully inquired into the mental competency of the Indian, signing the above will, the circumstances attending the execution of the will: the influence that may have induced its execution, and the names of those entitled to share in the estate under the law of descent in South Dakota: reasons for the disposition of the property proposed by the will, differing from disposition had the property descended by operation of law.

I respectfully forward this will with the recommendation that it be **disapproved, concurring with the recommendation of the examiner of Inheritance relative thereto.**

H M Tidwell
Supt. & Spl. Disb. Agent

DEPARTMENT OF THE INTERIOR
Office of Indian Affairs   OCT 25 1920

It is recommended that the within will of David Sits Poor, deceased Pine Ridge allottee No. 2817, be approved in accordance with the provisions of the Act of June 25, 1910 (36 Stat. L. 855-6), as amended by the Act of February 14, 1913 (37 Stat. L. 678), and the regulations of the Department.

Respectfully,
E B Meritt
Assistant Commissioner.

DEPARTMENT OF THE INTERIOR
Office of the Secretary   OCT 27 1920

The within will of David Sits Poor, deceased Pine Ridge allottee No. 2817 is hereby approved in accordance with the provisions of the Act of June 25, 1910 (36 Stat. L. 855-6), as amended by the Act of February 14, 1913 (37 Stat. L. 678), and the regulations of the Department

[Signed] ~~Alexander~~ T. Vogelsang
First Assistant Secretary

▲▼▲▼▲▼▲▼▲▼▲▼▲▼▲▼

<u>**PATRICK HENRY**</u>
Will of Patrick Henry
IN THE NAME OF GOD AMEN;

I, Patrick Henry, of the state of Nebraska, county of Knox, being of sound and disposing mind and memory but being uncertain of life and certain of the approach of death, and desiring to dispose of all my worldly possessions while I still have the power to do so, do make and declare this to be my last will and testament hereby revolking(sic) and annulling any and all wills heretofore made by me.

1.   I, Patrick Henry, do will and bequeath all my property, and all heirship property coming to me of which I am ah heir to, to Mark Henry and Lincoln Robinson, share and share alike.

In testamony whereof, I have set my hand and seal this 23d day of July 1918, at Santee, Knox County,. Nebraska.

HIS

Patrick Henry   (thumb print)

MARK

Signed, Sealed, published and declared this 23d day of July 1918, by the said Patrick Henry, in our presence, as and for his last will and testament, and at his request, and in his presence, and in the presence of each other we have hereunto subscribed our names as attesting witnesses.

Wyatt McNeilly, Santee, Nebr.
B J Young Santee Nebr.

Subscribed and sworn to before me this 23d day of July 1918.

B J Young
Notary public

Probate
S Y T
DEPARTMENT OF THE INTERIOR
Office of Indian Affairs   OCT 26 1920

It is recommended the within will be approved pursuant to the provisions of the Act of June 25, 1910 (36 Stat. L. 855-6), as amended by the Act of February 14, 1913 (37 Stat. L. 678).

Respectfully,
E B Meritt
Assistant Commissioner.

DEPARTMENT OF THE INTERIOR
Office of the Secretary   OCT 26 1920

The within will is hereby approved pursuant to the provisions of the Act of June 25, 1910 (36 Stat. L. 855-6), as amended by the Act of February 14, 1913 (37 Stat. L. 678).

A T Vogelsang
First Assistant Secretary

▲ ▼ ▲ ▼ ▲ ▼ ▲ ▼ ▲ ▼ ▲ ▼ ▲ ▼ ▲ ▼

TURNER ELK

WILL

I, Turner Elk, Ponca Indian Allottee #84 of the Ponca Tribe of Indians of Oklahoma, being now in poor health and strength of body yet sound in mind, but sensible of the uncertainty of life hereby declare this instrument to be my last will and testament, and hereby revoke all former testamentary dispositions of my estate heretofore made by me.

1st.   I direct payment of my just debts and funeral expenses.

2nd. I hereby give, devise and bequeath to any or each person that may be an heir to my estate under the laws of inheritence(sic), the sum of one dollar ($1.00).

3rd.   I hereby give, devise, and bequeath, jointly to my two daughters, Maggie E. Barnaby and Flora E. Poor Horse, the NE1/4 of the NE1/4 & Lot 4 in Section 29, Twp. 24 N of Range 3 East and the n1/2 of the NW1/4 of the NE1/4 in Section 18, Twp. 24, N., of Range 4 East, being my own original allotment, and the 31/2 of the NW1/2 of the NE1/4 in Section 18, Twp. 24 N., of Range 4 East being 20 acres which I inherited from my deceased daughter Daisy, and solely to my son John Elk the E1/2 of the NW1/4 in Section 29, Twp. 24 N., of Range 3 East being 80 acres which I inherited from my deceased daughter Daisy.

4th.   I hereby give, devise, and bequeath to my three children above named all my other property, real, personal, or mixed, wheresoever situated, each to share eaqwelly(sic).

5th.   This my last will and testament is made subject to the approval of the Secretary of the Interior and on the condition that my wife, Mary E. Elk, shall have the sole use and benefit of all my property until her death, otherwise this will to be of no effect.

IN WITNESS WHEREOF, I , Turner Elk, having had this instrument interpreted to me in the Ponca Indian Language by *Leonard Big Goose*, and educated Ponca Indian, have to this same instrument, affixed my right thumb print this 12th day of February 1920.   His

Turner Elk   (thumb print)
Testator   mark

SUBSCRIBED by Turner Elk in the presence of each of us the undersigned, and at the same time declared by him, to us, to be his last will and testament, and we, therefore, at the request of the testator, Turner Elk, in his presence and in the presence of each other, sign our names hereto this 12th day of February 1920.

Leonard Big Goose
Interpreter
Peter Leclair
W A Spencer

DEPARTMENT OF THE INTERIOR
Office of Indian Affairs   OCT 22 1920

The within will of Turner Elk, deceased Ponca allottee No. 84 and 84-A is hereby recommended for approval under the Act of June 25, 1910 (36 Stat. L. 855-6), as amended by the Act of February 14, 1913 (37 Stat. L. 678), and the Regulations of the Department.

Respectfully,
E B Meritt
Assistant Commissioner.

DEPARTMENT OF THE INTERIOR
Office of the Secretary   OCT 26 1920

The within will of Turner Elk, deceased Ponca allottee No. 84 and 84-A is hereby approved under the Act of June 25, 1910 (36 Stat. L. 855-6), as amended by the Act of February 14, 1913 (37 Stat. L. 678), and the Regulations of the Department.

A T Vogelsang
First Assistant Secretary

▲▼▲▼▲▼▲▼▲▼▲▼▲▼▲▼

Indian Wills, 1911 – 1921 Book 1
Records of The Bureau of Indian Affairs

<u>**JUDAH B WAR CHIEF**</u>

Yankton Agency
Greenwood, S. D.
Jan. 14th 1918

My dear only son Joseph Warchest and my dear wife Hetaninwin. I am in old age now I am 91 years of age and I am sick for over two months and I knew(sic) now that I am going to die passing away pretty soon now. I can tell you my dear son Joseph I will never live over three or four days now from this hour and on and so my dear son while I remember every thing and while I can talk I will gift you hafe(sic) of my money to you my dear son and the other hafe(sic) to my dear wife Hetaninwin. and I got eighty acres of heirship land of Tokaodana my son which die sometimes ago in the summer of 1901. I will gift you a forty acres of yours brother land which die and the other forty acres I will gift to you my dear wife Hetaninwin and also I bought a Liberty bond for five hundred dollars. this bond is a registered bond and I can say to you my dear son you got two nice daughters which are growing under you. I will gift this registered Liberty bond to my dear little grand daughters Lousia Warchief and Sophia Warchief. Lousia she can have hafe(sic) of this registered bond and the other hafe(sic) to Sophia. this is all I own and this is all I will say.

From yours dear loving father

Judah B War Chief

his (thumb print) *mark*

witness
Susan War chief

Probate
11700-19
96408-20
 M H W

DEPARTMENT OF THE INTERIOR
Office of Indian Affairs   OCT 15 1920

The within will of Judah B War Chief, deceased Yankton allottee No. 620, is hereby recommended for approval under the provisions of the Act of June 25, 1910 (36 Stat. L. 855-6), as amended by the Act of February 14, 1913 (37 Stat. L. 678), and the Regulations of the Department.

Indian Wills, 1911 – 1921 Book 1
Records of The Bureau of Indian Affairs

Respectfully,
E B Meritt
Assistant Commissioner.

DEPARTMENT OF THE INTERIOR
Office of the Secretary   OCT 21 1920

The within will of Judah B War Chief, deceased Yankton allottee No. 620, is hereby approved according to the provisions of the Act of June 25, 1910 (36 Stat. L. 855-6), as amended by the Act of February 14, 1913 (37 Stat. L. 678), and the Regulations of the Department.

Alexander Vogelsang
First Assistant Secretary

▲▼▲▼▲▼▲▼▲▼▲▼▲▼

ISAAC TATEBDOKA

LAST WILL AND TESTAMENT OF ISAAC TATEBDOKA
IN THE NAME OF GOD AMEN:

I, Tatebdoka, of the State of South Dakota, County of Charles Mix, being of sound mind and memory but being uncertain of life and certain of the approach of death, and desiring to dispose of all my worldly possessions while I have the power to do so, do make and declare this to be my last will and testament, thereby revoking and annulling any and all other wills heretofore made by me:

First:
I bequeath to my wife, Sarah Tatebdoka, that portion of my allotment where we now live on the Yankton Reservation, described as follows: the S/2 NE/4. Section 28, Twp. 95, Range 64, containing 80 acres.

Second:
I direct that all the remainder of my allotment and any inherited interests I may have, be sold by the Superintendent of the Yankton Indian Reservation and from the proceeds derived from this sale, after my just debts and funeral expenses are paid and a suitable monument erected to my grave, I give and bequeath to the following persons the amounts as follows: to my brother, Iron Night, I give the sum of $400.00; to my uncle, Minnecopa, I give the sum of $400.00; to my sister, Oyetenwin, I give the sum of $300.00; to my sister, Hanyetuwanwin, I give the sum of $300.00; to my niece Ellen Wachahnnka, I give the sum of $200.00; to my niece, Mrs. Frank Irving, I give the sum of

$200.00; to my niece, Wambdi, of the Rosebud Reservation, I give the sum of $200; to Jennette Manydogs, I give the sum of $300.00; and to my wife all the remainder of my property and money not otherwise disposed of both real and personal of which I may be possessed at the time of my death.

IN TESTEMONY(sic) WHEREOF; I have hereunto set my hand and seal this 28th day of April, 1920 at Wagner, South Dakota.

his
Isaac Tatebdoka   (thumb print)
mark

Signed, sealed, published, and declared, this 28th day of April, 1920, by the said Isaac Tatebdoka, in our presence as and for his last will and testament, and at his request and in his presence and in the presence of each other, we have hereunto subscribed our names as attesting witnesses.

E. G. Martin   Residing at Wagner, S. D.
Dan Yellowhair   Residing at Wagner, S. D.

79537-20
Probate
M H W
S Y T

DEPARTMENT OF THE INTERIOR
Office of Indian Affairs   OCT 21 1920
It is recommended that the within will be approved pursuant to the provisions of the Act of June 25, 1910 (36 Stat. L. 855-6), as amended by the Act of February 14, 1913 (37 Stat. L. 678).

Respectfully,
E B Meritt
Assistant Commissioner.

DEPARTMENT OF THE INTERIOR
Office of the Secretary   OCT 27 1920

The within will is hereby approved pursuant to the provisions of the Act of June 25, 1910 (36 Stat. L. 855-6), as amended by the Act of February 14, 1913 (37 Stat. L. 678).

Alexander Vogelsang
First Assistant Secretary

Indian Wills, 1911 – 1921 Book 1
Records of The Bureau of Indian Affairs

CODICIL TO LAST WILL AND TESTAMENT OF
ISAAC TATEBDOKE:

IN THE NAME OF GOD AMEN:

I, Isaac Tatebdoka, of the state of South Dakota and county of Charles Mix, being of sound mind and memory do declare this to be a codicil to my last will and testament executed April 28, 1920.

I desire the following change in the second part of my will: Instead of giving Jenette Manydogs the sum of $300.00 I desire that she be omitted from the will and the $300.00 divided among my beloved wife, Sarah Tatebdoka and Peter St Pierre and Frank Irving, share and share alike.

IN TESTEMONY WHEREOF: I have hereunto set my hand and seal this 16th day of June, 1920, at Wagner, South Dakota.

His
Isaac Tatebdoka   (thumb print)
Mark

Signed, sealed, published, and declared, this 16th day of June, 1920 by the said Isaac Tatebdoka, in our presence and as for a codicil to his last will and testament, and at his request and in his presence and in the presence of each other, we have hereunto subscribed our names as attesting witnesses.

E. T. Martin   Residing at Wagner, S. D.
Daniel Yellowhair   Residing at Wagner, S. D.

▲▼▲▼▲▼▲▼▲▼▲▼▲▼▲▼

KATHERINE KIRKIE (MRS. LEON KIRKIE)

LAST WILL AND TESTAMENT OF MRS.
LEON KIRKIE. Crow Creek,
South Dakota.

IN THE NAME OF GOD, Amen:

I, Katherine Kirkie, an allottee of the Yankton Indian reservation, in the state of South Dakota, being of sound mind memory and understanding, hereby make and publish this my last will and testament hereby revoking all wills by me heretofore made that is to say:

43

Indian Wills, 1911 – 1921 Book 1
Records of The Bureau of Indian Affairs

First: I direct that all my just debts and funeral expenses and the expenses of my last illness shall be paid as soon after my decease as shall be convenient.

Second: In case of my death, I desire that all that I am possessed of be divided among my three daughters Maggie, Sadie and Vera. The other two children on mine John and Lillian are now of age and able to take care of themselves. My husband Leon Kirkie and his three children from me I also leave out as he has treated me in a cruel and inhumane manner and I do not whish(sic) any of my property both real and personal go to him.

Third: These three children of mine that I have mentioned are now away to Phoenix, Arizona, for their health. If they should come back after my death, well and strong, I desire that they be placed in care of their grandmother Susan Strong, at Greenwood South Dakota, and that all monies that I may be possessed of at the time of my death be placed in the hands of the Superintendent of the Yankton Indian agency, for use of these three girls.

And Lastly: I am satisfied that the officers of the Department of the Interior of the United States will make proper provision for carrying into effect of this my last will and testament, and therefore, I have not appointed an executor to administer my estate.

In witness whereof I have set my hand and seal to this my last will and testament at my camp close to the home of Christine Eagle Dog on the Crow Creek reservation in the state of South Dakota, this 14th day of February 1920.

Peter W Lightfoot **Clerk, Crow Creek, S.D.** *Charles M. Bird*	Katherine Kirkie	Her (thumb print) Mark

Signed, sealed, published and declared by the said Katherine Kirkie, in our presence, as and for her last will and testament, and at her request and in her presence and in the presence of each other we have hereto subscribed our names as attesting witnesses thereto.

Peter W. Lightfoot   Charles M. Bird

79468-20
Probate
M H W

DEPARTMENT OF THE INTERIOR
Office of Indian Affairs   OCT 25 1920
It is recommended that the within will be approved pursuant to the provisions of the Act of June 25, 1910 (36 Stat. L. 855-6), as amended by the Act of February 14, 1913 (37 Stat. L. 678).

> Respectfully,
> *E B Meritt*
> Assistant Commissioner.

DEPARTMENT OF THE INTERIOR
Office of the Secretary   OCT 27 1920

The within will is hereby approved pursuant to the provisions of the Act of June 25, 1910 (36 Stat. L. 855-6), as amended by the Act of February 14, 1913 (37 Stat. L. 678).

> *A T Vogelsang*
> First Assistant Secretary

State of South Dakota)
                      : ss:
County of Buffalo   )

I, Katherine Kirkie, an allottee of the Yankton Indian reservation, in the state of South Dakota, after first being duly sworn, on oath, deposes and says that at the time that I made my will on the 14th instant, I forgot to mention that I desire that a team of ponies belonging to me and their harness I desire be given to Christine Eagle Dog, an allottee of this reservation, this I do for her care of me during my illness.

Witnesses: Her

                        Katherine Kirkie

Peter W Lightfoot   Mark
Martin Chase

Subscribed and sworn to before me this 16th day of February 1920.

                                        Peter W Lightfoot

DEPARTMENT OF THE INTERIOR
Office of Indian Affairs   OCT 25 1920

It is recommended that the within codicil be approved pursuant to the provisions of the Act of June 25, 1910 (36 Stat. L. 855-6), as amended by the Act of February 14, 1913 (37 Stat. L. 678).

Indian Wills, 1911 – 1921 Book 1
Records of The Bureau of Indian Affairs

Respectfully,
E B Meritt
Assistant Commissioner.

DEPARTMENT OF THE INTERIOR
Office of the Secretary   OCT 25 1920
The within codicil is hereby approved pursuant to the provisions of the Act of June 25, 1910 (36 Stat. L. 855-6), as amended by the Act of February 14, 1913 (37 Stat. L. 678).

A T Vogelsang
First Assistant Secretary

▲▼▲▼▲▼▲▼▲▼▲▼▲▼▲▼

ISADOR STRAIGHT TAIL

L A S T W I L L A N D T E S T A M E N T
of

____

IN THE NAME OF GOD, AMEN.

I, *Isador Straight Tail of Kenel, South Dakota* being of sound mind, memory and understanding, do hereby make and publish this my last will and testament, hereby revoking and annulling all wills by me heretofore made in manner and form following, that is to say.

First; I direct that all my just debts and funeral expenses and expenses of my last illness shall be paid by my executor, hereinafter named as soon after my decease as convenient;

Second; I give, devise and bequeath to *Susan Longchase my stepdaughter, the quarter section of my allotment No. 744 on which which*(sic) *the house now stands on the NE also the southeast quarter-one half section in all. To Larroy Douglass Afraid of Soldier I give the south west quarter and the remainder of my allotment I give to Stanislaus Thunderhawk Little Warrior.*

I also give and bequeath to James Alkire a cow and calf of bay color Branded 425.

To Mrs. Sebastian Whitehorse a bay cow and calf with shorter horns than above mentioned cow and calf Branded 425

To my brother Two Parents, I give one Black Mare, One Black Yearling and one Spring Colt - the last two being off springs of said Black Mare.

To William Bobtail of Cannon Ball, I give One Bay Mare also her Yearling and Spring Colts all branded 425 - all bays.

To Two Horse of Cannonball one Bay Mare also her yearling and spring colt Branded 425.

To Wizitewin of Poplar, Montana, One gray mare and colt already in her possession Branded 425.

To my wife's daughter, Susan Longchase I give One sorrel gelding Branded 425-I.D.   To Stephen Two Parents I give and bequeath One Bay Gelding, Branded 425.

To Bede Use His Arrows, I give and bequeath one Gray Gelding 4 yrs old Branded 509.

To James Alkire I give, one hayrake.   Tp Sam Ironhorn I give One Set Harness.   To Maurice Bearheart I give one Set of harness.   To Mrs. Maurice Bearheart I give One Cook Stove.   To Susan Alkire Longchase I give One set of harness.   To John Sack I give One Wagon.   To Mrs. Paul Ironwing I give one wagon.   To Mrs. Shavehead I give the log house and barn now standing on her land.

I wish a tombstone pointed out by me to Maurice Bearheart to be purchased and placed over my grave

Third;   All the rest and residue of my estate, both real and personal and mixed, I give, devise and bequeath to my lawful heirs as determined after my decease.

And. I do hereby nominate, constitute and appoint *Claude C Covey* executor of this my last will and testament.

In testimony whereof, I have set my hand and seal to this my last will and testament at *Kenel, S.D* , this *Twenty Ninth* day of *September,* in the year of our Lord one thousand, nine hundred and *Sixteen.*

And lastly, I hereby request *W. F. Mullally* to sign my name to this my last will and testament and witness the same.   his

Witness
- *W.F Mullally Principal*
-     *Kenel, S.D.*
- *Eugene Bearking*
-     *Kenel, S D*

Isador Straight Tail   mark
[Testator]

Signed, sealed, published and declared by said *Isadore Straight Tail of Kenel, S.D.* in our presence as and for *his* last will and testament. And at *his* request and in our presence and in the presence of each other, we have hereunto subscribed our names as attesting witnesses thereto.

W F Mullally	of	*Kenel, S. D.*
Eugene Bearking	of	*Kenel, S.D.*
Frank Halverson	of	*Kenel, S.D.*

DEPARTMENT OF THE INTERIOR
Office of Indian Affairs   OCT 21 1920
It is hereby recommended that the within will of Isidore Straight Tail or Isidore Straightail, deceased Standing Rock allottee No. 744, be approved in accordance with the provisions of the Act of June 25, 1910 (36 Stat. L. 855-6), as amended by the Act of February 14, 1913 (37 Stat. L. 678), and the Regulations of the Department. No rights of an executor will be recognized.

Respectfully,
E B Meritt
Assistant Commissioner.

DEPARTMENT OF THE INTERIOR
Office of the Secretary   OCT 27 1920
The within will of Isidore Straight Tail or Isidore Straightail, deceased Standing Rock allottee No. 744, is hereby approved in accordance with the provisions of the Act of June 25, 1910 (36 Stat. L. 855-6), as amended by the Act of February 14, 1913 (37 Stat. L. 678), and the Regulations of the Department. No rights of an executor will be recognized.

A T Vogelsang
First Assistant Secretary

▲ ▼ ▲ ▼ ▲ ▼ ▲ ▼ ▲ ▼ ▲ ▼ ▲ ▼ ▲ ▼

PEJUTAWIN OR SDINA SKANKIYA

Will of Pejutawin or Sdina Skankiya

IN THE NAME OF GOD AMEN:

I, Pejutawin or Sdina Skankiya, of the State of South Dakota, County of Charles Mix, being of sound and disposing mind and memory but being uncertain of life and certain of the approach of death and desiring of disposing of all my worldly possesions(sic) while I still have the power to do so, do make and declare this to be my last will and testament, hereby revoking and annulling any and other wills heretofore made by me.

First: I give devise and bequeath to my two granddaughters, Mary Yellowbird and Evelyn Bricks, that portion of my own allotment described as follows: the S1/2 of NE1/4 of NE1/4 of SECTION 19, Township 94, Range 64 West of 5th P.M., in South Dakota, each to share alike.

Second: I give devise and bequeath to my grand-son, Paul Wisapa and to my daughter Maggie S. Wisapa, that portion of my share in the estate of my deceased husband Skankiya, Allottee No. 408 each to share alike.

Third: I give devise and bequeath to my daughter Maggie S. Wisapa all the remainder of my property, both real and personal, of whatsoever nature, inherited, and otherwise, of which I may be possesed(sic) at the time of my death, after my just debts and funeral expenses are paid, and a monument errected(sic) at my grave.

IN TESTEMONY WHEREOF I have set my hand and seal this 25th day of May, 1920, at my home near Greenwood, South Dakota.

Her

Pejutawin or Sdina Skankiya

mark.

Signed, sealed, published and declare this 25th day of May, 1920, by the Pejutawin or Sdina Skankiya, in her presence as and for her last will and testement(sic) and at her request, and in her presence and in the presence of each other we have hereunto subscribed our names as attesting witnesses.

Homer Redlightning
S. M. Tutwiler

Indian Wills, 1911 – 1921 Book 1
Records of The Bureau of Indian Affairs

79648-20
Probate
M H W
S Y T

DEPARTMENT OF THE INTERIOR
Office of Indian Affairs   OCT 21 1920
It is recommended that the within will be approved pursuant to the provisions of the Act of June 25, 1910 (36 Stat. L. 855-6), as amended by the Act of February 14, 1913 (37 Stat. L. 678).

> Respectfully,
> *E B Meritt*
> Assistant Commissioner.

DEPARTMENT OF THE INTERIOR
Office of the Secretary   OCT 28 1920
The within will is hereby approved pursuant to the provisions of the Act of June 25, 1910 (36 Stat. L. 855-6), as amended by the Act of February 14, 1913 (37 Stat. L. 678).

> *A T Vogelsang*
> First Assistant Secretary

▲▼▲▼▲▼▲▼▲▼▲▼▲▼▲▼

<u>SICLIMMA SMITH</u>

Will of Siclimma Smith
Klamath Allottee #518

Supt. Watson -
This is my eanest(sic) wish and desire that whin(sic) I, Siclimma Smith die that my land and cattle shall be given to Mr. & Mrs. Peter Phillips, who have taken care of me for ten years.
Dated Klamath Reservation
> *Sept 1 1910 her mark*

Witness.
Mary E. Chiles
> *Minnie Hough*

DEPARTMENT OF THE INTERIOR
Office of Indian Affairs

Indian Wills, 1911 – 1921 Book 1
Records of The Bureau of Indian Affairs

The within will of Sic-lim-ma Smith, deceased Klamath allottee No. 518, is hereby approved under the Act of June 25, 1910 (36 Stat. L. 855-6), as amended by the Act of February 14, 1913 (37 Stat. L. 678).

>Respectfully,
>*E B Meritt*
>Assistant Commissioner.

DEPARTMENT OF THE INTERIOR
Office of the Secretary   OCT 27 1920
The within will of Sic-lim-ma Smith, deceased Klamath allottee No. 518, is hereby approved under the Act of June 25, 1910 (36 Stat. L. 855-6), as amended by the Act of February 14, 1913 (37 Stat. L. 678), and the Regulations of The Department.

>*A T Vogelsang*
>First Assistant Secretary

▲▼▲▼▲▼▲▼▲▼▲▼▲▼▲▼

<u>BA-MA-SHE-KWE or PE MA E KWE</u>

>COUNTY COURT
>*For* Ashland *County*

>IN PROBATE.

>*In the Matter of the Will of*
>Ba-Ma-She-Kwe *Deceased*

>CERTIFICATE OF PROBATE

>*Filed* 22 Sept *A.D.19* 19.
>James McCully.
>*County Judge*
>State of Wisconsin, County Court, Ashland County.

In the Matter of Ba-ma-she-kwe   )

         (In Probate.

    Deceased.   )

  An Instrument in writing purporting to be the last Will and Testament (and codicile thereto, if any) of Ba-ma-she-kwe of the Town of Sanborn (Village of Odanah), in said County, having been delivered into said Court:

And Charlotte Couture Thomas, of said County having presented to said Court a petition in writing, duly verified, representing among other things that said Ba-ma-she-kwe lately died testate, in said County, and praying that a time a place be appointed for proving said last will and testament (and codicile, if any), and that letters testamentary (or of administration with will annexed) in said matter be granted to Charlotte Couture Thomas;

THEREFORE, IT IS APPOINTED AND ORDERED, That said petition and the matters therein be heard, and proofs of said last will and testament (and codicile thereto, if any) be taken, at the Special Term of said Court, appointed to be held at the Court House, in the said County, in the City of Ashland, Wis. on the 2nd Tuesday of May 1918, at the opening of Court on that day, or as soon thereafter as said petitioner can be heard, when all concerned may appear and contest the probate of said instrument.

IT IS FURTHER ORDERED, That the time within which the creditors of said deceased shall present their claims against such estate for examination and allowance, be and hereby is fixed and limited to four months from the date hereof;

IT IS FURTHER ORDERED, That all claims and demands against said deceased be received at the Court House of said Court on any day hereafteruntil the expiration of the said four months and be examined and adjusted at the Special Term of said Court appointed to be held at the Court House in said County, in the City of Ashland on the 3rd Tuesday of August, 1918, at the opening of Court on that day, or as soon thereafter as the matter can be heard;

AND IT IS FURTHER ORDERED, That notice hereof be given to all persons interested, by publication thereof for three consecutive weeks in the Ashland Daily Press, a newspaper, published in said County, the first publication to be made within fifteen days from the date hereof.

Dated April 8th 1918.
> By the Court.
>> Geo. H. McCloud
>> Judge.

State of Wisconsin, County Court for Ashland County:

Indian Wills, 1911 – 1921 Book 1
Records of The Bureau of Indian Affairs

At a **Special** Term of the County Court within and for said County of **Ashland** begun and held at the **Court House** in the **City of Ashland** on the **22nd** day of **May** A.D. 1918.

IN THE MATTER OF THE WILL OF

Ba-Ma-she-kwe   Deceased.

STATE OF WISCONSIN,

Ashland County,   ss.

Ed Bachand and Jan La Fernier, two one of the subscribing witnesses, to the instrument propounded as the will of **Ba-Ma-She-Kwe** deceased, **each** being produced, sworn and examined............testified as follows:

I knew **Ba-Na-She*-Kwe** deceased in **her** life-time:

The instrument now shown to me, purporting to be his will, was signed by **her** at the **Odanah in County of Ashland, State of Wisconsin** on the **24th** day of **November 1916.**

She, at the same time, declared said instrument to be his will in my presence:

George H. McCloud - Ed Bachand and **Jan La Fernier** were present at the same time, and we severally subscribed our names to the same instrument, as witnesses, in the presence of said **Ba-Ma-She-Kwe**

The said **Ba-Ma-She-Kwe** was at the time of signing said instrument, above twenty-one years of age, and was of sound mind as I verily believe.

Sworn in open Court and subscribed before me, this

22nd day of **May 1918**

     Ed Bachand

     Jan LaFernier

H. P. Axelberg
County Judge

𝔖𝔱𝔞𝔱𝔢 𝔬𝔣 𝔚𝔦𝔰𝔠𝔬𝔫𝔰𝔦𝔫, ℭ𝔬𝔲𝔫𝔱𝔶 ℭ𝔬𝔲𝔯𝔱 𝔣𝔬𝔯 Ashland ℭ𝔬𝔲𝔫𝔱𝔶:

At a **Special** Term of the County Court within and for said County of **Ashland** begun and held at the **Court House** in the **City of Ashland** on the **22** day of **May** A.D. **1918.**

IN THE MATTER OF THE WILL OF

Ba-Ma-She-Kwe   Deceased.

The matter of hearing proofs of the instrument propounded by **Charlotte Couture Thomas** as the last will and testament of **Ba-Ma-She-Wa** deceased, having come on to be heard at this Term of said Court, and it appearing that due notice of the time and place of such hearing has been duly given as required by the order of the Court herein made on the **8th** day of **April** A.D. 1918

And the said proponent having appeared by **A. W. Sanborn** her attorney and **no one appearing in opposition and George H. McCloud and Ed Bachand appearing as witnesses** subscribing witness... to said instrument having been produced, sworn and examined .... upon consideration thereof the Court finds:

That said **Ba-Me-She-Kwe** died at **Odanah in the County Ashland** on the **16th** day of **January** A.D. 1918

That at the time of **her** death **she** was an inhabitant of **Odanah** in said County of **Ashland, Wisconsin**

That *after* the time hereinafter mentioned the said **Ba-Me-She-Kwe** was of full age and of sound mind;

That on the **24th** day of **November** A.D. 1916 at the **Village of Odanah in Ashland County Wisconsin** the said instrument was signed by said **Ba-Me-She-Kwe**

That said instrument was at the same time duly attested and subscribed by **George H. McCloud Ed Bachand and Jan LaFernier** who were competent witnesses thereto, in the presence of said **Ba-Me-She-Kwe** who at the same time declared it to be **her** Will;

That said instrument is the Last Will and Testament of said **Ba-Me-She-Kwe** deceased, in all things duly executed.

𝔚𝔥𝔢𝔯𝔢𝔣𝔬𝔯𝔢 𝔦𝔱 𝔦𝔰 𝔒𝔯𝔡𝔢𝔯𝔢𝔡 𝔞𝔫𝔡 𝔇𝔢𝔠𝔯𝔢𝔢𝔡, That said instrument be allowed and probate thereof granted, as the Last Will and Testament of said **Ba-Me-She-Kwe** deceased.

By the Court,

Dated **May 22 1918**   **H. P. Axelberg, acting**
County Judge

STATE OF WISCONSIN,⎫
                   ⎬ ss.
ASHLAND County.⎭

THE STATE OF WISCONSIN, To all to whom these presents shall come or may concern, and especially to **Charlotte Couture Thomas** of **Odanah, Ashland County, Wisconsin,** GREETING:

KNOW YE, That Whereas, **Ba-ma-she-kwe,** late of **Odanah, in the Town of Sanborn, in said County,** lately died testate, and being at the time of **her** decease an inhabitant of said County, by means whereof the proving and allowing of **her** Last Will and Testament, and granting administration of all and singular the goods, chattels, rights, credits and estate whereof she died possessed, and also auditing, allowing and finally discharging the accounts thereof, is within the jurisdiction of our County Court of said County, and...........

WHEREAS, on the **22nd** day of **May,** A.D. 1918, at **Ashland,** in said County, before the Hon **H.P. Axelberg, legally acting** Judge of our said County Court, the Last Will and Testament of the said **Ba-ma-she-kwe** was duly proved, allowed and admitted to probate; and ....

WHEREAS, **Charlotte Couture Thomas, the** executrix named in and by said Will, **is willing to accept said trust, and**

WHEREAS, it has been by the Court ordered that letters herein be issued to the said executrix without bond, in accordance with the terms of said will.

We, therefore, reposing full confidence in your integrity and ability, have granted, and by these presence do grant, the administration of all and singular the goods, chattels, rights, credits and estate of said deceased, and any way concerning ..... said Will, unto you the said **Charlotte Couture Thomas,**

Hereby authorizing and empowering you to take and have possession of all the real and personal estate, (except the homestead) of said deceased, and to receive the rents, issues and profits thereof, until said estate shall have been settled, or until delivered over by order of said Court to the devisees or heirs of said deceased; and to demand, collect, recover and receive all and singular the debts, claims, demands, rights and choses(sic) in action which to the said deceased while living and at the time of his death did belong.

And requiring you to keep in good tenantable repair all houses, buildings and fences on said real estate which may and shall be under your control; and to make and return into the said County Court, within three months, a true and perfect inventory of the real estate and of all the goods, chattels, rights, and credits of said deceased which shall come to your possession or knowledge; to administer, according to law, and the Will of said testator, all the goods, chattels, rights, credits and estate of said deceased which shall at any time come to your possession, or to the possession of any other person for you, and out of the same to pay and discharge all debts, legacies and charges chargeable on the same, or such dividends thereon as shall be ordered and adjudged by said Court; to render a just and true account of your administration to said Court within one year, and at any other time when required by said Court, and to perform all orders and judgments of said Court by you to be performed in the premises.

(Seal)	IN TESTIMONY WHEREOF, We have caused the
(County Court)	seal of our said County Court, to be hereunto
(Ashland County)	affixed.
(Wis.)	WITNESS, The Hon. **James McCully,** Judge of the said Court, at **Ashland,** in said County, this **22nd** day of **September,** A.D. **1919.**

James McCully   County Judge

The following is a copy of all enteries(sic) in the Minute Book of the County Court of Ashland County, Wisconsin, relative to the Matter of the Will of Ba-ma-she-kwe, Deceased.

April 8, 1918.

Frank B. Lamoreux filed an instrument purporting to be the last will and testament of Ba-ma-she-kwe, deceased.

Ordered that proofs of said instrument be heard at a special Term to be held on the second Tuesday of May, 1918, that creditors be allowed four months in which to present claims and that claims be heard at a Special Term to be held on the 3rd Tuesday of August, 1918.

May 22, 1918

Charlotte Couture, proponent, appeared by Sanborn, Lamoreux & Pray, her attorneys.

Geo. H. McCloud, subscribing witness, sworn and examined. Ed Bachand, subscribing witness, was sworn and examined.

Decree entered admitting Will to Probate.

Ordered that Charlotte Couture Thomas be appointed executrix without bond.

September 22, 1919.

Ordered that Letters testamentary issue to Charlotte Couture Thomas without bond, in accordance with the terms of the will.

Letters Testamentary issued to Charlotte Couture Thomas.

State of Wisconsin,)
      (ss.
Ashland County)

  I, James McCully, the County Judge of said County, do hereby certify that I have compared the foregoing copies with the original Will, Petition for probate thereof, Certificate of probate thereof, Order for hearing proofs of will and for hearing claims, Testimony of subscribing witness, Decree admitting will to probate, Letters testamentary, and all entries in the Minute Book of the County Court of said County relative to this proceeding, all in the Matter of the last Will and Testament of Ba-ma-she-kwe, Deceased, and that the same are true and correct copies of said original records, and of the whole thereof; that said originals now remain on file and of recrod(sic) in my office, and are by law required to be in my official custody.

In Testimony Whereof, I have hereunto set my hand and affixed the seal of the County Court of said County, at Ashland, this 22nd day of September, A.D. 1919.

James McCully

County Judge.

State of Wisconsin, In County Court, Ashland County

In the Matter of the Will of Ba-ma-she-kwe, Deceased.

Certified copy of Will, certificate of Probate thereof, Letters Testamentary, and other papers composing the record in said matter.

State of Wisconsin, County Court for Ashland County

In the Matter of the Will of)
                    (In Probate.
Ba-ma-she-kwe Deceased)

The petition of Charlotte Couture Thomas by Sanborn Lamoreux and Pray her attorneys respectfully shows:

That Ba-ma-she-kwe died at Odanah, Wis. on the 16th day of January A.D 1918.

That her domicile at the time was in town of Sanborn (Village Odanah) in said County of Ashland and State of Wisconsin;

On information and belief that Ba-ma-she-kwe left no personal property, of any value whatever and real estate of the probable value of six hundred Dollars, the annual rents and profits of which is of no value whatever and also left a will duly executed by here wherein your petitioner said Charlotte Courute(sic) Thomas is named as executrix which is herewith presented and propounded as her lat will and testament;

That said deceased left surviving no husband and no child but left the said Charlotte Couture Thomas the duly adopted child and heir at law of her the said

Ba-ma-she-kwe and that she the said Charlotte Couture Thomas is now of full age and under no disability and that none of the relatives of her the said Ba-ma-she-kwe are minors who have no general or testamentary guardian.

That your petitioner is the adopted child of her the said deceased.

Wherefore your petitioner prays that said will may be proved and allowed as the last will and testament of said Ba-ma-she-kwe deceased, and letters testamentary thereupon granted to Charlotte Couture Thomas.

SANBORN LAMOREUX & PRAY
Attorneys for Petitioner.

State of Wisconsin,)
                  (ss.
Ashland County.   )

Charlotte Couture Thomas being duly sworn on oath says that she is the petitioner above names; That she has he(sic) heard read the above and foregoing petition, and knows the contents thereof, and that the same is true to her own knowledge, excepting as to the matters therein stated on information and belief, and as to those matters she believes it to be true.

Subscribed and sworn to before me)
                          (Charlotte Couture Thomas
this 8th day of April A.D. 1918.   )

R R Hardy
Notary Public
Ashland County Wis.

I, Ba-ma-she-kwe, residing in the Village of Odanah, County of Ashland, State of Wisconsin, 80 years of age, and a member of the Bad River Band of Chippewa Indians, being of sound mind and memory, do make, publish, and declare this my last will and testament, hereby revoking all former wills, bequests, and devices by me made.

1. I give, devise, and bequeath to Charlotte Couture Thomas, 48 years of age, and a member of The Bad River Band of Chippewa Indians, living at Odanah, Ashland County, Wisconsin, who I am this day taking steps to legally adapt as my daughter, if the court will permit, my allotment held under the laws of the United States, together with the proceeds

therefrom; the allotment of my deceased husband, a sku da a mom and the proceeds therefrom; the allotment of my deceased son, William Rankin, and the proceeds therefrom; and all my other property of every description whatsoever, real, personal, and mixed, wherever the same may be, and however the title thereof may come to me.

2. I desire it to be known, and therefore state herein, that I have no children, brothers, sisters, or parents living, and the only descendant that I have living, so far as I know, is one Francis Rankin, who has been amply provided for with this world's goods, and is abundanny well off. I desire it further known, and therefore state herein, that the said Charlotte Couture Thomas has cared for and nursed me, and personally attended to my wants and needs for many years past, during which time I have been an invalid and unable to help myself; and she has during all of that time given her time and personal attention to me and my needs and wants, and has been all that a daughter could be to a mother, while my relatives, if there be any, have paid no attention to me or my necessities and needs. (NOTE:Antoine typed and crossed out on original)

3. I hereby appoint my legatee herein, Charlotte Couture Thomas, executrix of this my last will and testament, and direct that she be not required to give any bond as such executrix.

IN WITNESS WHEREOF, I have hereunto set my hand and seal this 24th day of November, A.D. 1916.

Ba-ma she kew (thumb mark) (SEAL)

The foregoing instrument was signed, sealed, published, and declared by the said Ma ba she kwe(sic) as and for her last will and testament in the presence of us, who, at her request, in her presence, and in the presence of each other, have hereunto subscribed our names as attesting witnesses, and said testatrix was then of sound and disposing mind and memory.

George H. Mc Cloud   Residing at Ashland, Wis.

Ed. Bachand   Residing at Odanah, Wis.

James LaFernere   Residing at Odanah, Wis.

The word "grand" was scratch and the word "Antoine" changed to "Francis" before this will was signed.

G. H. McCloud

DEPARTMENT OF THE INTERIOR
Office of Indian Affairs

The within Will of Ba mash e kwe or Pe ma e kwe, deceased Chippewa allottee 41, and bearing date of November 24, 1916, is hereby recommended for approval, and also that it be transmitted to the President of the United States for his approval in accordance with the provisions of the Treaty of September 30, 1854 (10 Stat. L. 1109)..

Respectfully,
E B Meritt
Assistant Commissioner.

DEPARTMENT OF THE INTERIOR
Office of the Secretary   OCT -5 1920

It is respectfully recommended that an instrument dated November 24, 1916, purporting to be the last will and testament of Ba mash e kwe or Pe ma e kwe, deceased Chippewa allottee 41, be approved in accordance with the provisions of the Treaty of September 30, 1854 (10 Stat. L. 1109).

John Sarton Payne
Secretary

THE WHITE HOUSE

APPROVED: *Woodrow Wilson*
7 October 1920

Woodrow Wilson
President.

Office Ind Affairs
Land Div.
Recorded in Misc. Deed Book Vol
14, page 396
Oct. 27, 1920

Indian Wills, 1911 – 1921 Book 1
Records of The Bureau of Indian Affairs

State of Wisconsin,
                } ss.
Ashland County,

BE IT REMEMBERED. That on the **22nd** day of **May A.D. 1918** at **Ashland** in said County, pursuant to notice duly given, as required by law, at a **Special** Term of the County Court of said County **the** subscribing witnesses to the last will and testament of **Ba-Ma-She-Kwe,** late of **Odanah** in said County, deceased, hereunto annexed, **were** produced and duly sworn and examined.

And the proofs having been heard before said Court and the Court having thereupon found that said instrument was in all things duly executed as **her** last will and testament by the said **Ba-Ma-She-Kwe**

Thereupon said instrument was by the order and decree of said Court duly allowed and admitted to probate, as and for the last will and testament of **Ba-Ma-She-Kwe,** deceased.

Ashland County
Court Seal

In Testimony Whereof, I have hereunto set my hand and affixed the seal of the County Court of said County, at **Ashland** this **22nd** day of **September** A.D. 1919

James McCully,   County Judge

▲▼▲▼▲▼▲▼▲▼▲▼▲▼▲▼

<u>OLIVE ROMANNOSE</u>

Last Will and Testament of Olive romannose(sic)

I, Olive Romannose, of Clinton, Okla. Being of sound and disposing mind and memory, and understanding, do make and publish this my last will and testament, hereby revoking all wills and codicils by me made.

First: I direct the payment of all my just debt and funeral expenses.

Second: I give, devise, and bequeath to my father Romannose Spottedhorse my allotment, the N.E. quarter of S. 24m T. 12N, E. 17W. This was originally my grandmothers, (Walking Woman) allotment.

Third: To my husband Lariet Comesevah, thirty dollars ($30.00).

Fourth: to my two children, Blaine and Lawrence, all my other property both real and personal, of which I may die posessed(sic), excepting such as herein before set forth.

In testimony hereof I have hereunto set my hand and seal at Clinton, Okla. this day of July 27th Ninetenn(sic) hundred and eighteen.

Olive Romannose

Witnesses:
Roland Croft
J.B. Ediger

Signed, published, and declared by Olive Romannose, the above named testator, as for her last will and testament, in our presence, who, at her request and in her presence, and in the presence of each other have hereunto subscribed our names as attesting witnesses.

Roland Croft
J.B. Ediger

Probate,
50260-20
  M H W

DEPARTMENT OF THE INTERIOR
Office of Indian Affairs   OCT 28 1920

It is hereby recommended that the within will of Olive Romannose, deceased Cheyenne allottee No. 82a, be approved according to the Act of June 25, 1910 (36 Stat. L. 855-6), as amended by the Act of February 14, 1913 (37 Stat. L. 678), and the Regulations of the Department.

> Respectfully,
> *E B Meritt*
> Assistant Commissioner.

DEPARTMENT OF THE INTERIOR
Office of the Secretary   NOV -1 1920

The within will of Olive Roman Nose, deceased Cheyenne allottee No. 82a, is hereby approved according to the Act of June 25, 1910 (36 Stat. L. 855-6), as

Indian Wills, 1911 – 1921 Book 1
Records of The Bureau of Indian Affairs

amended by the Act of February 14, 1913 (37 Stat. L. 678), and the Regulations of the Department.

A T Vogelsang
First Assistant Secretary

▲▼▲▼▲▼▲▼▲▼▲▼▲▼

<u>REE WOMAN or MARY MONICA or PALANINWIN</u>

LAST WILL AND TESTAMENT OF MARY MONICA or PALANINWIN OF DOUGLAS COUNTY, SOUTH DAKOTA.

I, Mary Monica or Palaninwin, being of sound and disposing mind and memory and free to act, and desirous of making an equitable and proper disposition of my property at my decease, do make, ordain, publish and declare this to be my Last Will and Testament in manner and form as follows:

FIRST: I hereby revoke and annul all former Wills by me made.

SECOND: I direct that all my just debts and funeral expenses be paid as soon after my decease as may be conveniently done.

THIRD: I give devise and bequeath to Louis Lefevre Primeau, of Armour, Douglas County, South Dakota the sum Seven Hundred Fifty ($750.00) Dollars Cash to him and his heirs and assigns forever.

FOURTH: I give, devise and bequeath to Rose Flavia Primeau of Armour, Douglas County, South Dakota, the sum of Seven Hundred Fifty ($750.00) Dollars cash, to him and his heirs and assigns forever.

FIFTH: To a young lady now about nineteen or twenty years of age, whose name I am not able to recall, she being the daughter and only living child of one Okute and residing on the Reservation near Fort Yates, North Dakota, the sum of Five Hundred ($500.00) cash to her and to her heirs and assigns forever.

SIXTH: All of the rest, residue and remainder of my estate remaining at the time of my death, over and above the forgoing bequests, I give, devise and bequeath to my three beneficiaries hereinbefore named, to be divided among the three equally, share and share, alike.

SEVENTH:I do hereby nominate, constitute and appoint John M. Carigman, of Fort Yates, North Dakota, executor of this my Last Will and Testament.

IN WITNESS WHEREOF, I have hereunto set my hand and seal this 16th day of September, A.D. 1910.

her

Mary Monica or Palaninwin (SEAL)

mark

This instrument was on the day of the date thereof, signed, published and declared by said testatrix, Mary Monica or Palaninwin, to be her Last Will and Testament, in our presence, who at her request have subscribed our names thereto as witnesses, in her presence and in the presence of each other.

Henry Keeler Residing at *Greenwood S.D.*
Alice D. Knapp Residing at *Armour, S.D.*

Probate 114633-16
83513-20; 81141-20

DEPARTMENT OF THE INTERIOR
Office of Indian Affairs   OCT 28 1920
It is hereby recommended that the within will of Ree Woman or Mary Monica or Palanawin, deceased Standing Rock Sioux allottee No. 874, be approved under the Act of June 25, 1910 (36 Stat. L. 855-6), as amended by the Act of February 14, 1913 (37 Stat. L. 678), and the Regulations of the Department.

Respectfully,
E B Meritt
Assistant Commissioner.

DEPARTMENT OF THE INTERIOR
Office of the Secretary   NOV -1 1920
The within will of Ree Woman or Mary Monica or Palanawin, deceased Standing Rock Sioux allottee No. 874, is hereby approved under the Act of June 25, 1910 (36 Stat. L. 855-6), as amended by the Act of February 14, 1913 (37 Stat. L. 678), and the Regulations of the Department.

A T Vogelsang
First Assistant Secretary

▲▼▲▼▲▼▲▼▲▼▲▼▲▼▲▼

SALLIE REUBEN

Round Valley Indian Agency
Covelo, Mendocino Co, Calif.
April 18, 1920

LAST WILL AND TESTAMENT OF
Sallie Reuben.

I, Sallie Reuben, Indian woman alloted(sic) on the Round Valley Indian Reservation, in the County of Mendocino, State of California, of the age of seventy (70) years, being of sound and disposing mind and memory, do make this my last will and testament, to-wit:-

FIRST:-   That all my just debts and funeral expenses shall be first duly paid:-

SECOND:- I give, devise and bequeath to my two grandsons, Leroy Duncan and Fillmore H. Duncan, both of the Round Valley Indian Reservation, my own allotment containing 5 acres and described as follows, to-wit:

The S1/2 of lot 56, Sec. 33, Twp. 23 N. Range 12 W. M.D.M., and the allotment of my late husband, Rueben, to which I have been declared the sole heir by the Secretary of Interior, under a decision rendered June 22, 1916, which allotment is more particularly described, as follows, to-wit:
The S1/2 of lot 57, Sec. 33, Twp. 23 N Range 12W. M.D.M., containing 10 acres,

Each of the aforesaid grandsons to inherit equally, share and share alike the 15 acres aforesaid and described.

It is my wish that my mountain allotment more particularly described as follows, to-wit:

NE1/4, of NW1/4 of NE1/4, S1/2 of NW1/2, NE1/4 & N1/2 of SW1/4 of NE1/4 & N1/2 of S1/2, SW1/4 of NE1/4, Sec. 33, Twp. 23 N, Range 12 W. M.D.M., containing 60 acres. Be sold by the Superintendent of the Round Valley Indian Agency, and the proceeds thereof apply to pay the expenses of my last illness and burial, and any residue thereof to be divided equally between the two aforesaid grandsons.

THIRD:-   I also give, devise and bequeath to my two grandsons, Leroy Duncan, and Fillmore H. Duncan, any other property personal or real, of which I maybe declared an heir after my death.

FOURTH:- I nominate and appoint the Superintendent of the Round Valley Indian Reservation, California, to be the executor of this my last will and testament, and request that he so act without giving bonds.

IN WITNESS WHEREOF I have hereunto set my hand and seal this 18th day of April, A.D. 1920.

WITNESSES: *Sallie Reuben*

Henry Henley
(Unable to read handwriting)

The foregoing instrument all being on the two pages upon which it is written, was at the date hereof, by the said Sallie Reuben, signed, sealed and published, and declared by her to be her last will and testament, in the presence of us who at her request and in her presence and in the presence of each other, subscribed our names as witnesses thereto.

> *Henry Henley*
> Residing at Covelo, California
> (Illegible handwriting)
> Residing at Covelo, California

▲▼▲▼▲▼▲▼▲▼▲▼▲▼▲▼

ALOPASTOB MARTIN

I, Alopastob Martin, of Taholah, Cheholis Co, Washington, allottee No. 338, of the Quinault Indian Tribe, and being of sound and disposing mind and memory and not acting under duress, menace, fraud, or undue influence of any person whatever, do make, publish and declare this my last will and testament in manner following that is to say:

First: I give to my
Daughter, Pausy Snell (Allottee No. 66)
Daughter, Lucy Hyasman (Allottee No 292)
Son   Colonel Martin (Allottee No 343)
Son   Henry Martin (Allottee No. 339)

Son   Edwin Martin (Allottee No 340)

In equal shares, all my property, both real and personal that I own at the present time or may own at the time of my death.

My reason for not giving anything to my Indian custom Husband, John Otook, Allottee No 52, is that we were not living together at the time I received my Allotment, also for the reason that we were not married according to the laws of the State of Washington.

In witness whereof: I have hereunto set my hand and seal this the Twentieth (20) day of September in the year of our Lord, One thousand nine hundred and fourteen (1914).

Alopastob Martin [her right thumb mark]

Witnesses to mark

We each sign this instrument in the presence of each other each one for himself and not one for the other.

G.C. White
Foress Guard
Taholah, Wash.

L C Gibson
Teacher
Taholah, Wash

I, Toby Saux, certify on honor that I acted as interpreter for Alopastob Martin in making his(sic) last Will and Testiment(sic); and that I read and interpreted the same that she thoroughly understood the contents thereof, and that I am not personally interested in same

Signed Interpreter, Toby Saux

DEPARTMENT OF THE INTERIOR
Office of Indian Affairs   JUL 17 1920
It is hereby recommended that the within will of Alopastob Martin, allottee No. 338 of the Taholah Tribe of Indians, be approved in accordance with the provisions of the Act of June 25, 1910 (36 Stat. L. 855-6), as amended by the Act of February 14, 1913 (37 Stat. L. 678), and the Regulations of the Department, but no rights of an executor will be recognized.

Respectfully,
E B Meritt
Assistant Commissioner.

Indian Wills, 1911 – 1921 Book 1
Records of The Bureau of Indian Affairs

DEPARTMENT OF THE INTERIOR
Office of the Secretary   NOV 11 1920

The within will of Alopastob Martin, allottee No. 338 of the Taholah Tribe of Indians, is hereby approved in accordance with the provisions of the Act of June 25, 1910 (36 Stat. L. 855-6), as amended by the Act of February 14, 1913 (37 Stat. L. 678), and the Regulations of the Department, but no rights of an executor will be recognized.

A T Vogelsang
First Assistant Secretary

▲▼▲▼▲▼▲▼▲▼▲▼▲▼▲▼

LAURA RED WOLF

LAST WILL AND TESTAMENT
of
Laura Red Wolf

In the name of God, Amen,

I, *Laura Red Wolf* of *Lodge Grass, Mont.* being of sound mind, memory, and understanding, do hereby make and publish this, my last will and testament, hereby revoking and annulling all wills by me heretofore made, in manner and form following, that is to say:

FIRST,   I direct that all of my just debts and funeral expenses, and expenses of my last illness shall be paid by my executor, as soon after my decease as convenient.

SECOND, I give, devise and bequeath to:

My mother Hazel Red Wolf, my sewing machine, washing machine and cook stoves. To my brother Chas Red Wolf, my bed mattress and spring.   To Three Tore Tops one old gray horse. To my Husband Harry Dont Mix all my land and one gray work horse. To my two children all the rest of any horses however many there are.

THIRD AND LASTLY, All the rest and residue of my estate both real, personal, and mixed, I give, devise and bequeath to my lawful heirs as determined after my decease.

In testimony whereof, I have set my hand and seal to this my last will and testament, at *Lodge Grass* , Montana, this *28th* day of *May 1919.*

Indian Wills, 1911 – 1921 Book 1
Records of The Bureau of Indian Affairs

Laura Red Wolf

Signed, sealed, published, and declared by said *Laura Red Wolf* in our presence, as and for *her* last will and testament, and at request and in our presence, and in the presence of each other, we have hereunto subscribed our names as attesting witnesses thereto.

> *C Haskins* of *Crow Agency* Montana
> *B P Cooper* of *Lodge Grass* Montana

Pro.
87910-19
R. T. B.

DEPARTMENT OF THE INTERIOR
Office of Indian Affairs   NOV 1920

It is hereby recommended that the within will of Laura Red Wolf, deceased Crow allottee No. 1507, be approved under the provisions of the Act of June 25, 1910 (36 Stat. L. 855-6), as amended by the Act of February 14, 1913 (37 Stat. L. 678), and the Regulations of the Department

> Respectfully,
> *E B Meritt*
> Assistant Commissioner.

DEPARTMENT OF THE INTERIOR
Office of the Secretary   NOV -5 1920

The within will of Laura Red Wolf, deceased Crow allottee No. 1507, is hereby approved under the provisions of the Act of June 25, 1910 (36 Stat. L. 855-6), as amended by the Act of February 14, 1913 (37 Stat. L. 678).

> *A T Vogelsang*
> First Assistant Secretary

▲▼▲▼▲▼▲▼▲▼▲▼▲▼▲▼

EDDIE RUSH, EDWARD RUSH or EVERYBODY LOOKS

LAST WILL AND TESTAMENT OF EVERYBODY LOOKS, EDWARD RUSH, or EDDIE RUSH

I, Everybody Looks, Edward Rush, or Eddie Rush, aged 30 years, a member of the Grosventre Tribe of Indians residing on the Fort Berthold

Indian Wills, 1911 – 1921 Book 1
Records of The Bureau of Indian Affairs

Reservation, North Dakota, being of sound mind and disposing memory, do hereby declare and publish this as my last will and testament, hereby revoking any and all other wills heretofore made by me.

1st. It is my wish, and I hereby will that all just debts, and the expense of my last illness and funeral be paid.

2nd. I hereby will, bequeathe(sic) and devise unto Nora Bird Bear, my wife, aged 24, all of my right, interest and title in and to the following described real-estate, of which I may die possessed, to-wit:
Allotment No. 1122-a, the SW1/4 of Sec. 25 and the SE1/4 Sec. 26, both in Twp. 148 N., Rge. 94, W 5th P.M., in North Dakota, containing a total of Three Hundred and Sixty acres, more or less according to the U.S. Government Survey thereof.

3rd. I further will and bequeathe(sic) unto the said Nora Bird Bear, two head of horses: One described as being 6 years old, branded V on left hip. sorrel geilding(sic). The other being a bay geilding(sic) years old 6 branded Flying Circle on left shoulder.

4th. I further will, devise and bequeathe unto the said Nora Bird Bear, the following described cattle: Ten head of cows age from 2 to 8 years old average weight 900# branded V connected H on right side.\

Five calves yearlings branded V connected H. on right side.

5th. I further will, devise and bequeathe unto the said Nora Bird Bear, my sled, wagon, sulky plow, 1 set harness, and all household goods, and all other property, real and personal, not otherwise here-in-after specified.

6th. I hereby will, bequeathe and devise unto Robert Rush, my own full brother, aged 34, all of my right, title and interest in and to my allotment No. 439, being the NW1/4 of the SW1/2, Sec. 27, Twp. 150 N., Rge. 91 W. 5th P.M., in North Dakota, containing 40 acres, more or less according to the United States Government Survey thereof.

7th. I hereby will, bequeathe and devise unto the said Robert Rush, all of my right, title and interest in and to an undivided One-sixth interest in the allotment of Strikes Many Women, No. 553, which is described as the E1/2 of the SW1/4 of Sec. 27, Twp. 150 N., Rge. 91, W. of the 5th P.M., in North Dakota, containing 80 acres more or less according to the U.S. Government survey thereof, which said one-sixth interest I inherited by Departmental finding L-H 22042-16.

8th. I further will, bequeathe and devise unto my said brother, Robert Rush, all of my right, title and interest in and to an undivided One-third interest in the allotment of Charging Enemy, No. 437, which is described as the SE1/4 of Sec. 14, Twp. 149 N., Rge. 91-W., 5th P.M., in North Dakota, containing 160 acres more or less according to the United States Government Survey thereof, which said one-third interest I inherited by Departmental finding L-H 22041-16.

9th. I further, will, bequeathe and devise unto my said brother, Robert Rush, all of my right, title and interest in and to an undivided One-half interest in the allotments of Francis (Frances) Enemy, or John Rush, as follows: Allotment No. 440, being the S1/4 of the SW1/4 of Sec. 27, Twp. 150 N, R. 91 W. 5th P.M., and containing 40 acres, more or less according to the United States Government Survey thereof; Allotment No. 1615, being the SE1/4 of the NE1/4 of Sec. 36, Twp. 140 N., of Rge. 94 Q. 5th P.M., and containing 40 acres more or less according to the United States Government Survey thereof; and Allotment No. 898-a, being the NW1/4 of Sec. 25, and he NE1/4 of Sec. 26, both in Twp. 148 N., of Rge. 94 W. of the 5th P.M. and containing 320 acres more or less according to the United States Government Survey thereof, all of said lands being in the State of North Dakota, which said one-half interest I inherited by Departmental finding L-H 18312-16.

10th. I further will, bequeathe and devise unto my said brother, Robert Rush, all of my right, title and interest in and to an un-divided One-third interest in the allotment of Singing or Joseph Rush, No. 441, being the NE1/4 of the NW1/4 of Sec. 23, Twp. 149 E., Rge. 91 W of the 5th P.M. in North Dakota, and containing 40 acres more or less according to the United States Government Survey thereof, which said 1/3 interest I inherited by Departmental finding L-H 22040-16.

11th. I further will, bequeathe and devise unto my said brother, Robert Rush, all of my right, title and interest in and to nine, (9), certain three-year-old steers, described as follows: average weight 900#, Branded V connected H on right side.

12th. I further will, bequeathe and devise unto my said brother, Robert Rush, two head of horses, described as follows: One Blue geilding(sic) 6 years old Branded (L. #.) on the right hip. One black Geilding 6 years old Branded V on left hip.

13th. I further will, bequeathe and devise unto my said brother, Robert Rush, all of the right, title and interest in and to the following described four head of cows and two calves:

Cows Age from 2 to 8 years. average weight about 900# branded V connected H on the right side. Calves yearlings, branded V connected H on the right side.

14th. I further will, bequeathe and devise unto my said brother, Robert Rush, all of my right, title and interest in and to a certain dwelling house, located on the allotment of John Rush No. 440, which is described as follows: Frame house, two stories, 4 rooms.

15th. I further will, bequeathe and devise unto my said brother, Robert Rush, one set of harness.

It is my last wish, and will, that items Nos. 6 to 15 be carried out, in consideration that my said brother, Robert Rush, assume all of my debts.

Witness: *Louis Baker*
             Frank L Brennan

Dated at Independence this 14th day of May, A.D., 1920.

We *Louis Baker* and *Frank L Brennan* on this 14th day of May, A.D., 1920, were requested to sign the foregoing instrument as witnesses to the last will and testament of the above mentioned Eddie Rush by the said Eddie Rush making such request and he at the same time declaring it to be his last will and testament, and publishing it as such he signing his name in our presence and we subscribing thereto, each for himself, in his presence, and in the presence of each other.

Louis Baker	aged	*41*
Frank L. Brennan	aged	*36*

Subscribed and sworn before me this 14th day of May, A.D. 1920.

James W. Hall
Notary Public, McClean County North Dakota
My Commission expires July 2, 1924.

Probate
83504-20
J M P

DEPARTMENT OF THE INTERIOR
Office of Indian Affairs   NOV 4 1920

The within will Eddie Rush, deceased allottee Nos. 439, 1669, and 1122a of the
Ft. Berthold Agency, is hereby recommended for approval pursuant to the Act of
June 25, 1910 (36 Stat. L. 855-6), as amended by the Act of February 14, 1913
(37 Stat. L. 678).

> Respectfully,
> *E B Meritt*
> Assistant Commissioner.

DEPARTMENT OF THE INTERIOR
Office of the Secretary   NOV -5 1920

The within will of Eddie Rush, deceased allottee Nos. 439, 1669, and 1122a of
the Ft. Berthold Agency, is hereby approved pursuant to the Act of June 25,
1910 (36 Stat. L. 855-6), as amended by the Act of February 14, 1913 (37 Stat.
L. 678).

> *A T Vogelsang*
> First Assistant Secretary

▲▼▲▼▲▼▲▼▲▼▲▼▲▼▲▼

LOOKING FOR WATER

LAST WILL AND TESTAMENT OF LOOKING FOR WATER
- - - - - - - - -

I, Looking for Water, aged 57, a member of the Grosventre Tribe residing
in the Shell Creek District of the Fort Berthold Reservation, in North Dakota,
being of sound mind and disposing memory, do make, declare and publish this
as my last will and testament, hereby revoking and annulling any and all other
wills heretofore made by me.

1st.   I do hereby will and bequeath and devise unto my grandson,
Henry Drags Wolf, or Has Wings, aged 13, a member of the Grosventre tribe
residing in the Shell Creek District on the Fort Berthold Reservation, North

Dakota, all of my right, title and interest in and to the following described real estate:

Allotment No. 521-a, the West One-half (1/2) of Section Thirty-four (34), in Township One Hundred fifty-two (152), North of Range Ninety-four (94), containing Three Hundred and Twenty, (320), acres more or less according to the United States Government Survey, thereof all being West of the 5th P.M. in North Dakota. I also leave all my money, from leases or otherwise, to the said Henry Drags Wolf.

IN WITNESS WHEREOF, I have hereunto affixed my thumb mark, as evidence that I publish and declare this to be my last will and testament, on this Twenty-seventh day of September, A.D., 1917.   *Her*

Looking For Water (thumb print)

mark

State of North Dakota,   )

                     : ss.

County of McLean.   )

I, Looking For Water, having made the foregoing will, and being of lawful age, and being first duly sworn upon oath depose and say that I have in the said will designated my daughter, Prairie Dog Woman, aged 51, she being the mother of Henry Drags Wolf or Has Wings, to whom I have willed my land, solely because I desired that Henry Drags Wolf or Has Wings have my land, I having raised him from a child, and he being crippled in his limbs in such a manner as to preclude the possibility of ever being able to support himself by manual labor, and there is no ill feeling between Prairie Woman, my daughter, and myself, by my leaving my land to her cripples boy, who is also my grandson.   *Her*

Looking For Water

mark

Subscribed and sworn to before me this 27th day of Sept. 1917

Fred Huber
Notary Public.
My Commission expires Jan 17th 19*20*

On the 27th day of September, A.D., 1917, at Elbowoods, N.D., we, the undersigned, were requested to sign the foregoing instrument, as witnesses to the will of Looking For Water, by the said Looking For Water, making such request, and she at the same time declaring it to be her last will and testament, and publishing it as such, she signing her name in our presence, and we subscribing thereto, each for himself; in her presence, and in the presence of each other.

Frank H. Makineau
Elbowoods, N.D.
Thomas Smith
Elbowoods, N.D.

DEPARTMENT OF THE INTERIOR
Office of Indian Affairs   OCT 28 1920

It is hereby recommended that the within will of Looking For Water, Deceased Fort Berthold allottee #207, 521a, be approved under the Act of June 25, 1910 (36 Stat. L. 855-6), as amended by the Act of February 14, 1913 (37 Stat. L. 678), and the Regulations of the Department.

Respectfully,
E B Meritt
Assistant Commissioner.

DEPARTMENT OF THE INTERIOR
Office of the Secretary   NOV -6 1920

The within will of Looking For Water, Deceased Fort Berthold allottee #207, 521a, is hereby approved under the Act of June 25, 1910 (36 Stat. L. 855-6), as amended by the Act of February 14, 1913 (37 Stat. L. 678).

A T Vogelsang
First Assistant Secretary

▲▼▲▼▲▼▲▼▲▼▲▼▲▼▲▼

<u>TIPI</u>

Standing Rock Agency
North Dakota
Nov. 21, 1911

To whom it may concern:
*   I, Tipi, of Fort Yates, N. Dak, being of sound mind and memory, do make and declare this to be first and my last will and testament, to wit:*
<u>*First*</u>*: I give and bequeath one mare & one colt and a harness to Abbie M. White, my grand-daughter.*

<u>*Second*</u>*: I give and bequeath one mare and the increase to Mrs. Fig-moccasin of Cannon Ball*

Third: I give and bequeath one Lumber wagon to the husband of Abbie M White.

Fourth: I give and bequeath all of my land to the following person as heir to my estate, that the land shall be sold and divide the proceeds equally among the following persons, Mary Gayton, Abbie M White, William Gayton, John Gayton, Samuel Gayton, Charles Gayton, Alice Archambault, Emma Bruce and James Gayton.

In witness whereof I have hereunto set my thumb mark on this 21st day of November, 1911
Witnesses:

Thomas Frosted

Benjamin White

her

Tipi (thumb print)

mark

Probate
85117--20
M H W

DEPARTMENT OF THE INTERIOR
Office of Indian Affairs   NOV 3 1920

It is hereby recommended that the within will of Tipi, deceased Standing Rock Sioux allottee No. 1702, be approved according to the Act of June 25, 1910 (36 Stat. L. 855-6), as amended by the Act of February 14, 1913 (37 Stat. L. 678), and the Regulations of the Department.

Respectfully,

E B Meritt

Assistant Commissioner.

DEPARTMENT OF THE INTERIOR
Office of the Secretary   NOV -6 1920

The within will of Tipi, deceased Standing Rock Sioux allottee No. 1702, is hereby approved under the Act of June 25, 1910 (36 Stat. L. 855-6), as amended by the Act of February 14, 1913 (37 Stat. L. 678).

A T Vogelsang

First Assistant Secretary

▲▼▲▼▲▼▲▼▲▼▲▼▲▼▲▼

RATTLES GOING or BELLE RISE UP

LAST WILL AND TESTAMENT
of
Rattles Going or Belle Rise Up

In the name of God, Amen,

I, *Rattles Going or Belle Rise Up* of *Lodge Grass, Mont* being of sound mind, memory, and understanding, do hereby make and publish this, my last will and testament, hereby revoking and annulling all wills by me heretofore made, in manner and form following, that is to say:

<u>FIRST</u>, I direct that all of my just debts and funeral expenses, and expenses of my last illness shall be paid by my executor, as soon after my decease as convenient.

<u>SECOND</u>, I give, devise and bequeath to:
My husband Robert Rise Up (40) Forty acres of my land described as the $SW\frac{1}{4}$ $SE\frac{1}{4}$ Sec 12, Twp 7 R 36 E. To my mother, Sings In The Woods (40) Forty-acres of my land described as the $SE\frac{1}{4}$ $SW\frac{1}{4}$ Sec 12 Twp 7 R 36E. To my daughter Lizzie Bull Noose (80) acres grazing land described as the $E\frac{1}{2}$ $NW\frac{1}{4}$ Sec 14 Twp 7 R 36 E. To my husband Robert Rise Up my mowing machine and loose rake, also my heating stove. To my daughter Lizzie Bull Noose my buggy and cook stove. All money to my credit in Crow Agency or elsewhere to be equally divided between my husband Robert Rise Up and my Daughter Lizzie Bull Noose

<u>THIRD AND LASTLY</u>, All the rest and residue of my estate, both real, personal, and mixed, I give, devise, and bequeath to my *Husband Robert Rise Up*.

In testimony whereof, I have set my hand and seal to this my last will and testament, at *Lodge Grass*, Montana, this *3rd* day of *November 1919*.

Rattles Going or
Belle Rise Up Her Mark (thumb
print)

Signed, sealed, published, and declared by said *Belle Rise Up Rattles Going* in our presence, as and for *her* last will and testament, and at request and in our presence and in the presence of each other, we have hereunto subscribed our names as attesting witnesses thereto.

J P Cope	of	*Lodge Grass* Montana
George Hill	of	*Lodge Grass* Montana

Probate
57951-20
R T B

DEPARTMENT OF THE INTERIOR
Office of Indian Affairs

It is recommended that the within will of Rattles Going or Belle Rise Up, Crow allottee No. 1236, be approved under the Act of June 25, 1910 (36 Stat. L. 855-6), as amended by the Act of February 14, 1913 (37 Stat. L. 678), and the Regulations of the Department.

Respectfully,
E B Meritt
Assistant Commissioner.

DEPARTMENT OF THE INTERIOR
Office of the Secretary   NOV -6 1920
The within will of Rattles Going or Belle Rise Up, Crow allottee No. 1236,

is hereby approved according to the Act of June 25, 1910 (36 Stat. L. 855-6), as amended by the Act of February 14, 1913 (37 Stat. L. 678), and the Regulations of the Department.

A T Vogelsang
First Assistant Secretary

▲▼▲▼▲▼▲▼▲▼▲▼▲▼

GOOD CEDAR LEAN

WILL

IN THE NAME OF GOD AMEN:

I, **Good Cedar Lean** Fort Peck allottee No. **533** residing at **Drew** Montana, being of sound mind but of feeble health and realizing the uncertainty of life, and not acting under fraud, duress, menace or undue influence, do this **26** day of **Jan 1919**, make, publish and declare the following to be my last will and testament.

First:

I give, device and bequeath to **my beloved daughter, Good Nest Drum, /2 of my grazing land described as NW /4 of sec. 7 in lots 1 and 2. My team of horses and wagon that I also give to my daughter, Good Nest Drum, described land is in T. 30 N.R. 54 E. P.M.M.**

Second:

I give, devise and bequeath to **my beloved nephew, Samuel Conger, /2 of my grazing land described as SW/4 of sec 7, T. 30 N. R. 54 E. in lots 3 and 4.**

Third:

I give, devise and bequeath to **my beloved neice**(sic), **Mrs. Chas Thompson, my share of interest in my deceased husband's grazing land described as lot 1 in NW/4 of sec 18, and /E./2 of NW/4 of Sec. 18. T. 30 N. R. 54 E. P.M.M. and NW/4 of SE/4 of sec 26, T. 28N. R. 54 E. being allotment of Lean No. 2 allottee No. 532. deceased.**
****

4th. I give, devise and bequeath to my two beloved grandchildren, Hazel Drum and Ethel Drum, daughters of Good Nest Drum, my forty acre allotment described as SE/4 of NE/4 of Sec. 1. T. 27 N. R. 54 E. Any monies held in trust for me at the Office of Supt. Fort Peck agency, after my death shall be devided(sic) between my heirs, all lands mentioned in this will are situated on the former Fort Peck Reservation.

I hereby appoint E. D. Mossman, Supt. of Fort Peck Agency, or his successor in office, as executor of my estate.   *Her*

                              Good Cedar Lean (thumb print)
                              Fort Peck allottee No. *533   mark*

Witness:

            Alvin Warrior Farmer Brockton
            Ralph Spotted Bull   Brockton

We, the undersigned, hereby certify on our honor that neither of us are related in any way to the testat….., that we were both present and witnessed the signature of the testat…. to the above instrument in one page which … read and fully understood before signing as ….. was apparently of sound mind and signed the same of … own free will and accord stating that …. wishes were duly set forth.

*Alvin Warrior Farmer
Ralph Spotted Bull*

DEPARTMENT OF THE INTERIOR
Office of Indian Affairs   OCT -1 1920

The within will of Good Cedar Lean, deceased Fort Peck Yankton Sioux allottee No. 533 of the Fort Peck Reservation, is recommended for disapproval, in accordance with the provisions of the Act of June 25, 1910 (36 Stat. L. 855-6), as amended by the Act of February 14, 1913 (37 Stat. L. 678).

Respectfully,
E B Meritt
Assistant Commissioner.

DEPARTMENT OF THE INTERIOR
Office of the Secretary   NOV -5 1920
The within will of Good Cedar Lean, deceased Fort Peck Yankton Sioux allottee No. 533 of the Fort Peck Reservation, is hereby disapproved in accordance with the provisions of the Act of June 25, 1910 (36 Stat. L. 855-6), as amended by the Act of February 14, 1913 (37 Stat. L. 678), and the Regulations of the Department.

A T Vogelsang
First Assistant Secretary

▲▼▲▼▲▼▲▼▲▼▲▼▲▼

MRS. THROWING WATER (BLUE)

LAST WILL AND TESTAMENT OF

Mrs. Throwing Water (Blue)

    I, Mrs. Throwing Water (Blue), of Colony, Oklahoma, in the County of Washita, State of Oklahoma, being of sound and disposing mind and memory and understanding, do make and publish this my last will and testament, hereby revoking and annulling all wills and codicils by me made.

    FIRST: I give, devise and bequeath to my son, Andrew Throwing Water, the Northwest 1/4 of Sec. 26. Tp. 10 N., R. 16 W of P.M., containing 160 acres, same being my own allotment.

Indian Wills, 1911 – 1921 Book 1
Records of The Bureau of Indian Affairs

IN TESTIMONY WHEREOF, I have hereunto set my hand and seal at Colony, in the County of Washita, State of Oklahoma, this twenty-eighth day of January, Nineteen Hundred and Sixteen.

Her

WITNESSES: *Mrs. Throwing Water (Blue)* (thumb print)

George Beuh
Interpreter Colony, Okla.
C. Frances McDonald
Clerk Colony, Okla.

mark

Signed, published and declared by Mrs. Throwing Water (Blue) the above names testator, as and for her last will and testament in our presence who, at her request and in her presence, and in the presence of each other, have hereunto subscribed out(sic) names as attesting witnesses.

Witnesses *Long Hair* *His* (thumb print) *mark*
George Beuh *Little Bird* *His* (thumb print) *mark*
Interpreter Colony Okla
C. Frances McDonald
Clerk Colony Okla.

DEPARTMENT OF THE INTERIOR
Office of Indian Affairs   OCT 28 1920

The within will of Mrs. Throwing Water (Blue), is hereby recommended for approval, in accordance with the Act of June 25, 1910 (36 Stat. L. 855-6), as amended by the Act of February 14, 1913 (37 Stat. L. 678).

Respectfully,
E B Meritt
Assistant Commissioner.

DEPARTMENT OF THE INTERIOR
Office of the Secretary   NOV -5 1920

The within will of Mrs. Throwing Water (Blue), is hereby approved in accordance with the Act of June 25, 1910 (36 Stat. L. 855-6), as amended by the Act of February 14, 1913 (37 Stat. L. 678).

A T Vogelsang
First Assistant Secretary

▲▼▲▼▲▼▲▼▲▼▲▼▲▼▲▼

Indian Wills, 1911 – 1921 Book 1
Records of The Bureau of Indian Affairs

<u>JULIA WOLFE</u>

LAST WILL AND TESTAMENT

OF

Julia Wolfe

IN THE NAME OF GOD, AMEN.

I, **Julia Wolfe** OF **Fort Yates, North Dakota** BEING OF SOUND MIND, MEMORY AND UNDERSTANDING, DO HEREBY MAKE AND PUBLISH THIS MY LAST WILL AND TESTAMENT, HEREBY REVOKING AND ANNULLING ALL WILLS BY ME HERETOFORE MADE, IN MANNER AND FORM FOLLOWING, THAT IS TO SAY.

FIRST; I DIRECT THAT ALL MY JUST DEBTS AND FUNNERAL(sic) EXPENSES, AND EXPENSES OF MY LAST ILLNESS SHALL BE PAID BY MY EXECUTOR HEREINAFTER NAMED AS SOON AFTER MY DECEASE AS CONVENIENT;

SECOND; I GIVE, DEVISE AND BEQUEATH TO *Mrs. Elma Caddotte $300.00 from money to the credit of my estate from my father's estate.*

To Clara Many Wounds for services & care rendered during my illness $10.00.

To Nellie Shoenhut for services & care rendered during my illness $6.00.

To Mrs. Anna DuBray, for services & care rendered during my illness $50.00.

To my sister, Evelyn Brown Wolfe, born 1806, and my brother Henry Wolfe, Born 1811, the rest and residue of my estate both real, personal and mixed, share & share alike.

THIRD; ALL THE REST AND RESIDUE OF MY ESTATE, BOTH REAL, AND PERSONAL AND MIXED, I GIVE, DEVISE AND BEQUEATH TO MY LAWFUL HEIRS AS DETERMINED AFTER MY DECEASE.

AND, I DO HEREBY NOMINATE, CONSTITUTE, AND APPOINT *Philip Deloria* EXECUTOR TO THIS MY LAST WILL AND TESTAMENT.

IN TESTIMONY WHEREOF, I HAVE SET MY HAND AND SEAL TO THIS MY LAST WILL AND TESTAMENT, AT **Fort Yates, North Dakota** THIS **3rd** DAY OF **December**, IN THE YEAR OF OUR LORD ONE THOUSAND, NINE HUNCRED AND *Seventeen*.

AND LASTLY, I HEREBY REQUEST .... TO SIGN MY NAME TO THIS MY LAST WILL AND TESTAMENT AND WITNESS THE SAME.

Julia Wolfe
TESTATOR OR TESTATRIX

SIGNED, SEAL, PUBLISH AND DECLARED BY SAID *Julia Wolfe* IN OUR PRESENCE, AS AND FOR *her* LAST WILL AND TESTAMENT. AND AT *her* REQUEST AND IN OUR PRESENCE AND IN THE PRESENCE OF EACH OTHER, WE HAVE HEREUNTO SUBSCRIBED OUR NAMES AS ATTESTING WITNESSES THERETO.

J O Giegold   OF   *Fort Yates, N.D.*
Chas Picard   OF   *Fort Yates, N.D.*

DEPARTMENT OF THE INTERIOR.

The above will is hereby disapproved, under the Act of June 25, 1910 (36 Stat. L., 855-856), as modified by the Act of February 14, 1913 (97 Stat. L. 678).

First Assistant Secretary

DEPARTMENT OF THE INTERIOR
Office of Indian Affairs   NOV 3 1920

The within will of Julia Wolfe, deceased Standing Rock allottee No. 136, is hereby recommended for approval, according to the Act of June 25, 1910 (36 Stat. L. 855-6), as amended by the Act of February 14, 1913 (37 Stat. L. 678).

Respectfully,
E B Meritt
Assistant Commissioner.

DEPARTMENT OF THE INTERIOR
Office of the Secretary   NOV 9- 1920

The within will of Julia Wolfe, deceased Standing Rock allottee No. 136, is hereby approved according to the Act of June 25, 1910 (36 Stat. L. 855-6), as amended by the Act of February 14, 1913 (37 Stat. L. 678).

S G Hopkins
Assistant Secretary

▲▼▲▼▲▼▲▼▲▼▲▼▲▼▲▼

<u>ELIZABETH WHITEMAN</u>

LAST WILL AND TESTAMENT

I, Elizabeth Whiteman, being of sound mind and memory do hereby make, publish and declare this to be my last will and testament, hereby revoking any and all wills heretofore made by me,

First, I bequeath to my Grand Daughter Angelique Archambeau, the forty acres of land where I now live described as the South-West quarter of the North East quarter of Sec. Thirty-six T. Ninety-four N.R. Sixty-four West together with the buildings thereon, and also lot 798 according to the Yankton Survey all located in Charles Mix County So. Dak.

Second, I bequeath to my younger grand daughter Eveline Archambeau lot 778 and 799 according to the Yankton Survey all located in Charles Mix County So. Dak.

Third, I bequeath to my husband Redbird lot 779 according to the Yankton Survey located in Charles Mix County So. Dak.

Fourth, I bequeath to my Step-Daughter Eliza Gullikson the sum of $100.00 in cash.

Fifth, I direct that from any funds that may be to my credit under the supervision of the Superintendent of the Yankton Indian Agent(sic) at the time of my death. that the sum of $200.00 be used in the purchase of two $100. Liberty Loan United States Bonds, and that these bonds be purchased one each, in the name of my two grand daughters Angelique and Eveline Archambeau.

Sixth, I direct that all the residue of my property both real and personal of whatever nature of which I may be possessed at the time of my death, and after my just debts and funeral expenses have been paid, and a monument erected to my grave to cost not less than two hundred dollars, be divided equally between my two grand daughters Angulique(sic) Archembeau(sic) and Eveline Archambeau.

Witnessed my hand and seal this 18th day of April 1918 at Greenwood, Charles Mix County, South Dakota.

Elizabeth Whitman

SIGNED, SEALED, PUBLISHED AND DECLARED this 18th day of April 1918 as and for my last will and testament and at her request and in her presence and in the presence of each other, have signed as attesting witnesses.

Emmett E McNully Farmer Wagner, So.Dak.
Dan Yellowhair Greenwood, So.Dak.

Probate

S Y T

DEPARTMENT OF THE INTERIOR
Office of Indian Affairs   NOV 4 1920

The within will of Elizabeth Whiteman, deceased Yankton Sioux allottee No. 10, is hereby recommended for approval in accordance with the Act of June 25, 1910 (36 Stat. L. 855-6), as amended by the Act of February 14, 1913 (37 Stat. L. 678).

Respectfully,
E B Meritt
Assistant Commissioner.

DEPARTMENT OF THE INTERIOR
Office of the Secretary   NOV -5 1920

The within will of Elizabeth Whiteman, deceased Yankton Sioux allottee No. 10, is hereby approved in accordance with the Act of June 25, 1910 (36 Stat. L. 855-6), as amended by the Act of February 14, 1913 (37 Stat. L. 678).

A T Vogelsang
First Assistant Secretary

▲▼▲▼▲▼▲▼▲▼▲▼▲▼▲▼

DANIEL WILSON or TATEWANYAGMANI

LAST WILL AND TESTAMENT.

IN THE NAME OF GOD, Amen.

I, Daniel Wilson, or Tatewanyagmani, of the county of Roberts and State of South Dakota, being of sound mind and memory, and considering the uncertainty of this frail and transitory life; do hereby make, ordain, publish, and declare this to be my Last Will and Testament, hereby revoking any and all Wills by me made at any time heretofore.

First, it is my will, and I do so order and direct that all of my just debts and funeral expenses be paid as soon after my decease as conveniently may be.

Second, After the payment of such funeral expenses and debts by my legal executor, I give, devise and bequeath to my beloved sister, Rdajojiyewin, 40 acres of land described as the NE/4 of NE/4, Section 9-126-52; same being a part of my original allotment and it is estimated at $1600.00

Third, to my nephew, John Isiacs, I give the sum of $100.00 from any funds to my account.

Fourth, To my nephew, Frank Isiacs, I give and bequeath all of my lands described as follows; 40 acres, the remainder of my original allotment, dexceibed(sic) as NW/4 of NW/4, Section 10-126-52, same being worth about $1600.00;   Also my undivided interest in and to the estate of my decreased sister, Darna Oyatedutawin, described as Lot 3 of NW/4, Sec. 2-126-52; and SW/4 of NE/4; and SE/4 of N W/4; and Lot 2 of NW/4, all of Section 18-125-52. Allotment No. 425. *Value $4200.00*

Fifth, it is my request that all my other property, real and personal, be divided among my lawful heirs, according to the law governing the division of such estates.

In testimony whereof, I have hereunto subscribed my name and affixed my seal this 12th day May, in the year of our Lord one thousand nine hundred and eighteen.

his
Daniel Tatewanyagmani (thumb print)
mark

This instrument was, on the day of the date thereof, signed, published and declared by the said testator, Daniel Wilson, to be his Last Will and Testament in our presence, who at his request, have subscribed our names thereto as witnesses, in his presence, and in the presence of each other.

Adam Hehn　　　Residing at Sisseton, S. Dak.

E. A. Ceminger　　Residing at Sisseton, S. Dak.

I hereby approve the foregoing Last Will and Testament of *Daniel Wilson* this 12th day of May, A. D. 1918.

W. E. Dunn
Superintendent, Sisseton,
Agency, South Dakota

Probate
14266-21
R T B

DEPARTMENT OF THE INTERIOR
Office of Indian Affairs   MAY 7 1921

It is recommended that the within will of Daniel Wilson Tatewanyagmani, Sisseton allottee No. 1027, be approved under the Act of June 25, 1910 (36 Stat. L. 855-6), as amended by the Act of February 14, 1913 (37 Stat. L. 678).

Respectfully,
E B Meritt
4-FBM-21   Assistant Commissioner.

DEPARTMENT OF THE INTERIOR
Office of the Secretary   MAY 9 1921

The within will of Daniel Wilson Tatewanyagmani, Sisseton allottee No. 1027, is hereby approved under the Act of June 25, 1910 (36 Stat. L. 855-6), as amended by the Act of February 14, 1913 (37 Stat. L. 678).

E B Finney
First Assistant Secretary

▲▼▲▼▲▼▲▼▲▼▲▼▲▼

<u>WILLIAM ABE SOMERS (SOMMERS)</u>

Will and Testament

I, William Abe Somers of Canton, Oklahoma, a Cheyenne Indian, being of sound mind and memory, do now make and publish this my last Will and Testament; that is to say

I give, devise and bequeath all my property, real, personal and mixed to my wife, Mah-sach-ta, absolutely, with full power to sell and convey the same.

I do not give any of my property to my half brothers and half sister as I have been of no expense to them and they have never visited me in my sickness; while my wife has taken care of me and spent hundreds of her money on me I want partly to re-imburse(sic) her.

The lands I am interested in as an heir are the allotments of Short Neck, my father, and Esther Short Neck, my half sister, both under the Cheyenne and Arapaho Agency.

William Abe Somers

Signed, sealed, published and declared by the said testator as and for his last Will and Testament; and we at the request and in his presence, and in the presence of each other, have hereto subscribed our names as witnesses. Written on two (2) sheets. Dated October 7, 1919-

McClain Badgley
Ebenezer Kingsley
Susie Tobacco
Otto Hill

DEPARTMENT OF THE INTERIOR
Office of Indian Affairs   MAY -7 1921

It is recommended that the within will of William Abe Sommers, be approved under the Act of June 25, 1910 (36 Stat. L. 855-6), as amended by the Act of February 14, 1913 (37 Stat. L. 678).

Very truly yours,
E B Meritt
Assistant Commissioner.

DEPARTMENT OF THE INTERIOR
Office of the Secretary   MAY -7 1921

The within will of William Abe Sommers, is hereby approved under the Act of June 25, 1910 (36 Stat. L. 855-6), as amended by the Act of February 14, 1913 (37 Stat. L. 678).

SG Hopkins
Assistant Secretary

(NOTE: The above Will was listed twice)

▲▼▲▼▲▼▲▼▲▼▲▼▲▼

LUCY WALKINGBULL, LUCY MEADE or LUCY GOODHORSE

LAST WILL AND TESTAMENT OF LUCY WALKINGBULL?(sic), DEVILS LAKE SIOUX INDIAN.

In the name of God, Amen:

I, Lucy Walkingbull, of Fort Totten, North Dakota, being of sound mind, memory and understanding, and not under any stress of circumstances, do hereby make and publish this my last will and testament, revoking all wills heretofore made by me, in manner and form following, that is to say:

First, I direct that all my just debts and the expenses in connection with my last illness and burial shall be paid as soon after my death as convenient.

Second, I give, devise and bequeath all my inherited interests in lands on the Devils Lake reservation to my father, Michael Mead, my mother Nancy Mead and my son Benedict Walkingbull, all to have share and share alike.

Third, it is my will that my husband, George Walkingbull, shall inherit no part of my estate for the reason that he has habitually failed to support me, and is now away from me and neglecting me in my illness.

Fourth, I give, devise and bequeath all my personal property, including any money to my credit in the Fort Totten Agency office, to my father mother and son in equal shares.

And lastly, I do hereby nominate, constitute, and appoint my father Michael Mead as executor of this my last will and testament.

In testimony whereof, I have set my hand and seal to this, my last will and testament, at Fort Totten, North Dakota, this eighteenth day of May, in the year of our Lord, 1920.

Her
Lucy Walkingbull (thumb print)
Mark

Signed, sealed, published and declared by the said Lucy Walkingbull, in our presence, as and for her last will and testament, and at her request and in her presence, and in the presence of eachother(sic), we have hereunto subscribed our names as attesting witnesses thereto.

> *Frank Christy*
> *Sam Young*
> *Martin Strait*

Pro.
62439-20
R T B
DEPARTMENT OF THE INTERIOR
Office of Indian Affairs   MAY -5 1921

It is recommended that the within will of Lucy Walking Bull or Lucy Meade or Lucy Goodhorse, deceased un-allotted Devils Lake Sioux Indian be approved under the Act of June 25, 1910 (36 Stat. L. 855-6), as amended by the Act of February 14, 1913 (37 Stat. L. 678).

> No executor to be recognized
> Very truly yours,
> *E B Meritt*
> Assistant Commissioner.

DEPARTMENT OF THE INTERIOR
Office of the Secretary   MAY 6- 1921

The within will of Lucy Walking Bull or Lucy Meade or Lucy Goodhorse, deceased un-allotted Devils Lake Sioux is hereby approved under the Act of June 25, 1910 (36 Stat. L. 855-6), as amended by the Act of February 14, 1913 (37 Stat. L. 678). No executor to be recognized

> *SG Hopkins*
> Assistant Secretary

MAUDE GOODROCK FOURSPIDER

Will Maude Goodrock Fourspider

RECEIVED
FEB 19 1921
14385

I, Maude Goodrock Fourspider, widow, aged 72, allottee 347 of Fort Peck Indian Agency, Poplar, Mont, residing at Blair, Sheridan Co, Mont. being of sound and disposing mind do declare this my last will and testament and it is my wish and I hereby bequeath at my death that my land in Sheridan Co, Ft. Peck Reservation said and described as follows

320 acres allotment, the E1/2 Sec 34- T 32-52 and 40 acres

105434

shall be shared equally, one third to each between the following persons, being Goodwoman Hunter, my sister, allottee 428, aged 70 yrs, and Robert Buckelk, allottee 120, aged 48 yrs, both Fort Peck Agency Indians and residing in Blair, Montana, and Meade Steele, my grandson aged 26 yrs, allottee #922 of Fort Peck Indian Agency, Mont.

To my niece Esther Buckelk, Indian of Blair, Mont, aged 1 year I give my wagon, harness, and my black horse 10 yrs.

Signed and delivered at Blair, Mont, Sheridan Co, This First day of September 1916.

her

In presence of   *Maude Goodrock Fourspider* (thumb print)

right thumb

Frederick E Farrell, Farmer US DD.
Richard Crowe
Interpreter, Govt. herder
Ft. Peck Resv. Mont.

DEPARTMENT OF THE INTERIOR
Office of Indian Affairs
Washington, D.C.   APRIL 18 1921

It is recommended that the within will be disapproved in accordance with the act of June 25, 1910 (36 Stat. L. 855-6), as amended by act of February 14, 1913 (37 Stat. L. 678).

Respectfully,
E B Meritt
Assistant Commissioner.

DEPARTMENT OF THE INTERIOR
Office of the Secretary
Washington, D.C.   APRIL 29 1921

The within will is hereby disapproved in accordance with the act of June 25, 1910 (36 Stat. L. 855-6), as amended by the act of February 14, 1913 (37 Stat. L. 678).

SG Hopkins
Assistant Secretary

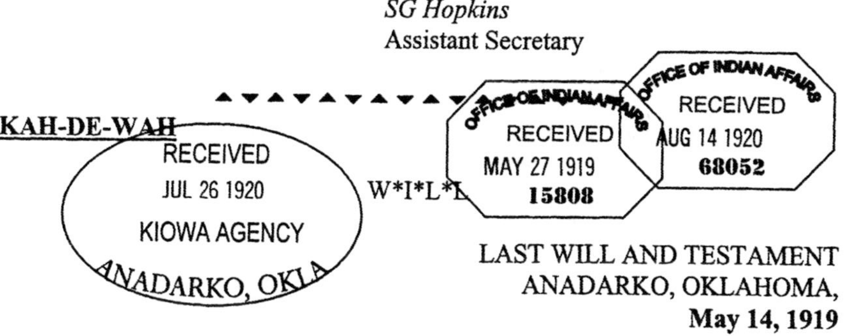

LAST WILL AND TESTAMENT
ANADARKO, OKLAHOMA,
May 14, 1919

I, Kah-de-wah, Wichita Indian allottee 249 of Anadarko, Oklahoma, Caddo County, Oklahoma, sound in body and mind, but sensible of the uncertainty of life and desiring to make disposition of my property and affairs while in health and strength do hereby make publish and declare the following to be my last will and testament, hereby revoking and cancelling(sic) all other or former wills by me at any time made.

First- I direct the payment of my just debts and funeral expenses.

Second- I give and devise, in equal shares, to my beloved grand-children, Ella Lee; Spencer Lee; Blaine Lee; all of my trust allotment of land comprising the South-Half of the South West Quarter (S1/2 of SW1/4) Section 5 and the South-Half of the South East Quarter (S1/2 of SE1/4) Section 6- all in township 8 North of Range 10 W. I. M. in Caddo County, Oklahoma. This lease is known upon the rolls of the Interior Department as Wichita Indian allotment 249 and was allotted to me by the United States and the deed thereto is still held in trust by the United (Page stopped here.)

The divisees(sic) in this devise, namely said grand-children, Ella Lee; Blaine Lee and Spencer Lee and the children of my daughter Mis-se-nah, Wichita Indian allottee 429 and of my son-in-law Whit Lee, Wichita Indian allottee 517, these grand children have not received an allotment of land and I am making this devise giving them each a one third (1/3) undived(sic) interest in and to my allotment for the purpose of giving them the benefit of a trust allotment of land.

Third- I give and devise all the rest, residue and remainder of all of my property, real of(sic) personal, of which I may die possed(sic), to the following persons, in equal shares; (a) to be(sic) beloved wife, De-ah-sun-ne-ah-cut-tah-dish, Wichita Indian allottee 427; (b) to my beloved daughter and only living child, Mis-se-nah, Wichita Indian allottee 429; (c) to my grand-daughter Anna Shau-acer, Wichita Indian allottee 448; (d) to my beloved grand son Ned Greely, an un-allotted Wichita Indian upon the Kiowa reservation in Oklahoma; the last named benificiary(sic) and grand-son is the son of Horace Greely, Wichita Indian allottee 428, who was my son and of Martha Frazier, Wichita Indian allottee 537, my daughter-in-law. This last devise to my said wife and only living child and of my(sic) grand-children Anna Shau-acer, and Ned Greely, is to include all of my right, title and interest in and to the following real-estate; to-wit, 1st, the Fr. North West Quarter of Section 30-Township 8, North of Range 10 W. I. M. Caddo County, Oklahoma. This land was originally allotted to Say-is-sick, Wichita Indian allottee 251, now deceased. In the decree of the Department (L. H. 85506-14 E G T) I was declared the sole heir of said estate; 2nd, the North West Quarter of Section 20-Township 8 North of Range 13 W, I. M. in Caddo County, Oklahoma. This is Wichita Indian allotment 565, allotted to Ase-tor, now deceased, in the decree of the Department (L. H. "416874 E G T") I was declared an heir in and to said estate to the extend of 4/12 (four twelfth) there-of—3rd—the North East Quarter of Section 9-Township 8 North of 10 W. I. M. in Caddo County, Oklahoma. This is Wichita Indian allotment 250, originally allotted to He-dates-char-a-dis-kad-de-wah, now deceased- in the decree of the Department (L H-85507-14 E G T) I was declared the sole heir of said estate.

I hereby declare my said wife and said daughter, grand-daughter and grand-son, named in paragraph three hereof, as devisees and beneficiaries, to be my sole heirs at law, were I to die intestate, now.

This will is made subject to the approval of the Secretary of the Interior.

IN WITNESS WHEREOF, I, Kah-de-wah, have to this my last will and testament, consisting of 5 sheets of paper, subscribed my name this *14* day of *May* 1919.

his

Kah-de-wah   *(thumb print)*

thumb mark

Witnesses:
W. A. Wilkin
  Anadarko, Okla.
Mary Wilkin
  Anadarko, Okla.

Subscribed by Kah-de-wah in the presence of us the undersigned, and at the same time declared by him to us to be his last will and testament and we thereupon at his request and in his presence and in the presence of each other, sign our names hereto as witnesses near Anadarko, Caddo County, Oklahoma, this *15* day of *May*

> *W A Wilkin*
> *Anadarko, Okla.*
> *Mary Wilkin*
> *Anadarko, Okla.*

INTERPRETERS CERTIFICATE

I, *Dennis Warden* hereby certify on honor that I acted as interpreter during the execution of the foregoing last will and testament of Kah-de-wah;   that I interpreted clearly and fully all the contents of said will to the said testator prior to the execution of said instrument and that all the provisions therein contained met with his full approval and consent and that said will was drawn strictly in accordance with his desires and directions.

I further certify that I speak both the Wichita Indian and the English languages fluently and that I have no interest whatsoever in this matter.

Signed this *15* day of *May* 1919.

> *Dennis Warden*

DEPARTMENT OF THE INTERIOR
Office of Indian Affairs   APR 19 1921
It is recommended that the within will Kah-de-wah be approved under the Act of June 25, 1910 (36 Stat. L. 855-6), as amended by act of February 14, 1913 (37 Stat. L. 678).

> Respectfully,
> *E B Meritt*
> Assistant Commissioner.

DEPARTMENT OF THE INTERIOR
Office of the Secretary   MAY 4- 1921
The within will of Kah-de-wah is hereby approved under the Act of June 25, 1910 (36 Stat. L. 855-6), as amended by the act of February 14, 1913 (37 Stat. L. 678).

> *SG Hopkins*
> Assistant Secretary

▲ ▼ ▲ ▼ ▲ ▼ ▲ ▼ ▲ ▼ ▲ ▼ ▲ ▼ ▲ ▼

MRS. PO PO MARTIN or SHAUB-WOT

DEPARTMENT OF THE INTERIOR
UNITED STATES INDIAN SERVICE

Nett Lake, Minn.
March 12 – 1920

Last will and testament of Mrs. Po Po Martin

I (Shaubwot) Mrs. Po Po Martin, being of sound and devising mind, and believing my death to be near, do hereby make this my last will and testament. My property I dispose of as follows.

All land and real estate in my own allotment and my shares in inherited lands, which are on record in the Indian office I give and bequeath to my son Joseph Martin and my daughter Ke-way-be-mans-eke or Mrs. Charlie Farmer, to be shared equally between them.

And because of the fact that my daughter Mrs. Chas. Farmer has cared for me in my last days it is my will that shall have three fifths of all moneys now to my credit as well as 3/5 of all moneys to be derived from sale of timber now being cut on my land.

The remaining two fifths of all moneys is to go to my son Joseph Martin.

Witnesses		*her*
	Shaub wot	*x*
Frank H. Pequette	*Mrs. Po Po Martin*	*mark*
A H Spears		

I wrote the above will and I made the insertion of "3/5 of" in the above will in order to make it clear that that portion of the money to be derived from sale of timber on her allotment was to go to her daughter, Mrs. Charlie Farmer. I did not notice the difference in will until later. (See my letter)   A   H Spears Physician in charge

DEPARTMENT OF THE INTERIOR
Office of Indian Affairs   APR 28 1921

It is hereby recommended that the within will of Mrs. Po Po Martin, deceased Chippewa allottee No. 85, be approved in accordance with the provisions of the

Act of June 25, 1910 (36 Stat. L. 855-6), as amended by act of February 14, 1913 (37 Stat. L. 678).

Respectfully,
E B Meritt
Assistant Commissioner.

DEPARTMENT OF THE INTERIOR
Office of the Secretary   APR 28 1921

The within will of Mrs. Po Po Martin, deceased Chippewa allottee No. 85, is hereby approved in accordance with the provisions of the Act of June 25, 1910 (36 Stat. L. 855-6), as amended by the act of February 14, 1913 (37 Stat. L. 678).

SG Hopkins
Assistant Secretary

▲▼▲▼▲▼▲▼▲▼▲▼▲▼▲▼

<u>PETER DRIFT</u>   COPY

Last Will and Statement

I, Peter Drift, of Nett Lake, Minn., in the county of Koochiching state of Minnesota, being of sound mind and memory, and considering the uncertainties of life, do here make publish and declare this to be my last will and testament.

First, I order and direct that my just debts and funeral expenses shall be paid as soon after my decease as conveniently may be, said debts and expenses to be paid from my real and personal property of which I may be seized at the time of my decease.

Second, I give, devise and bequeath to my daughter, Jane Connor, wife of H. A. Connor, all my allotment on the bois Fort Reservation, and all other properties that I may possess at my death, after my just debts are paid as above specified.

Any and all former wills made by me are hereby revoked.

In testimony whereof, have hereunto subscribed my name and affixed my seal this 21st day of September, 1914.

Peter Drift, his mark

Witnesses to Mark

Frances Reese (Sgd.)
    Nett Lake, Minn.

H. A. Connor (Sgd.)
    Nett Lake, Minn.

This instrument was, on the date thereof, signed, published and declared by the said testator, Peter Drift, to be his last will and testament in our presence, who at his request have subscribed our names thereto as witnesses in his presence and in the presence of each other."

Tom Fisher   Residing at Nett Lake, Minn, -- and Indian.

                     Residing at Nett Lake, Minn.--- an Indian.

Signed in the presence of

Frances Reese   (Sgd.)

H. A. Connor   (Sgd.)

Subscribed and sworn to before me at Nett Lake, Minn., this 21st day of Sept., 1914.

               (Signed)   Albert B. Reagan
                            Supt. & Special Disb. Agt.

PROBATE
28066-1921
  E G T

DEPARTMENT OF THE INTERIOR
Office of Indian Affairs   EGT   APR 20 1921

It is hereby recommended that the within will of Peter Drift, deceased Chippewa allottee No. 703, be approved in accordance with the provisions of the Act of June 25, 1910 (36 Stat. L. 855-6), as amended by act of February 14, 1913 (37 Stat. L. 678).

Respectfully,

(SGD) E. B. Meritt

Assistant Commissioner.

DEPARTMENT OF THE INTERIOR

Office of the Secretary APR 29 1921

The within will of Peter Drift, deceased Chippewa allottee No. 703, is hereby approved in accordance with the provisions of the Act of June 25, 1910 (36 Stat. L. 855-6), as amended by the act of February 14, 1913 (37 Stat. L. 678).

     (SGD) SG Hopkins

4-MH-11   Assistant Secretary

▲▼▲▼▲▼▲▼▲▼▲▼▲▼▲▼

MEDICINE HORSE

I, *Medicine Horse* , living at the Big White River Day-School Camp, in the County of Tripp, State of South Dakota, being of sound mind and disposing memory, do hereby make, publish, and declare this my last will and testament, hereby revoking all wills, codicils, bequests and devises of whatever nature previously made by me.

I hereby appoint as Executors of this my Will:

Joseph Thunder	of	*Houston, So. Dok.*(sic)
George Scott	of	*Houston, So. Dok.*(sic)

and I will and direct that said Executors be not required to give any bond or security for the faithful discharge of said trust.

After all my lawful debts are paid, I give, devise and bequeath to my (this was blank).   All of my personal property of every kind whatsoever, and wheresoever situated.

I also bequeath, give and devise to my *Grand-daughter Effie Ethel Pretty Voice Hawk* my allotments of land and any other property that may hereafter be aquired(sic) by me.

IN WITNESS WHEREOF, I have hereunto set my hand and seal this *first* day of *February* A. D., nineteen hundred and thirteen.

his
Medicine Horse (thumb print)
mark

Signed, sealed, published and declared by the said *Medicine Horse* as and for his last will and testament, in the presence of us, who, at his request, in his presence, and in the presence of each other, have hereunto subscribed our names as attesting witnesses to said instrument.

Henry Bradley
Kennebee, S.D.
Isaac Belletyoan
Winner, So. Dok.
Jack King
Winner So. Dak.

DEPARTMENT OF THE INTERIOR
Office of Indian Affairs

It is hereby recommended that the within will be approved under the provisions of the Act of June 25, 1910 (36 Stat. L. 855-6), as amended by Act of February 14, 1913 (37 Stat. L. 678).

E. B. Meritt
Assistant Commissioner.

DEPARTMENT OF THE INTERIOR
Office of the Secretary   APR 7 1921

The within will is hereby approved under the provisions of the Act of June 25, 1910 (36 Stat. L. 855-6), as amended by the Act of February 14, 1913 (37 Stat. L. 678).

SG Hopkins
Assistant Secretary

▲▼▲▼▲▼▲▼▲▼▲▼▲▼

JAMES WILSON

WILL

OFFICE OF INDIAN AFFAIRS
RECEIVED
APR 14 1920
32185

IN THE NAME OF GOD, AMEN: I, **James Wilson** age 74, an Indian of the Nez Perce Indian Reservation, Idaho, now residing at **Stites** Idaho, being of sound mind and disposing memory, and not acting under duress, menace, fraud, or undue influence, of any person, whatsoever, do hereby make, publish and declare this my LAST WILL AND TESTAMENT, in the manner following, that is to say:

First: I direct that my body be decently buried with proper regard to my station in life, and the circumstances of my estate.

Second: I direct that my funeral expenses and expenses of my last illness be paid from any funds belonging to my estate, or in the custody of the Superintendent of the Nez Perce Indian Reservation, Lapwai, Idaho.

Third: I will and bequeath to Eleanor G. Anderson all the money deposited to my credit with the Superintendent of the Nez Perce Indian Agency of which I die possessed.

I have no relatives that I now of, and if I do, I disinherit them for the reason that they have never cared for me. I will and bequeath all of which I may die possessed to Eleanor G. Anderson for the reason that she has always cared for me and looked after my interests.

My own allotment has been sold, and I have no inherited interests.

In witness whereof, I have hereunto put my hand and seal this **8th** day of **April 1920.**

his
James Wilson   (thumb print)
mark

The foregoing instrument was on the date hereof signed, sealed, published and declared by said **James Wilson** to be his LAST WILL AND TESTAMENT, in the presence of us, and at his request and in h...(sic) presence, and in the presence of each other, we have subscribed our names as witnesses on this **8th** day of **April 1920.**

Corbett Lawyer
Leta Brock

Probate
32185-20
 J W H

Indian Wills, 1911 – 1921 Book 1
Records of The Bureau of Indian Affairs

DEPARTMENT OF THE INTERIOR
Office of Indian Affairs
The within will of James Wilson, deceased allottee No. 1036, of the Nez Perce tribe, is respectfully recommended for approval, pursuant to the provisions of the Act of June 25, 1910 (36 Stat. L. 855-6), as amended by Act of February 14, 1913 (37 Stat. L. 678).

Respectfully,
E. B. Meritt
Assistant Commissioner.

DEPARTMENT OF THE INTERIOR
Office of the Secretary   MAR 30 1921

The within will of James Wilson, deceased allottee No. 1036, of the Nez Perce tribe is hereby approved pursuant to the provisions of the Act of June 25, 1910 (36 Stat. L. 855-6), as amended by the Act of February 14, 1913 (37 Stat. L. 678).

SG Hopkins
Assistant Secretary

▲▼▲▼▲▼▲▼▲▼▲▼▲▼▲▼

<u>SCOLDS</u>

Last Will and Testament
of
IN THE NAME OF GOD, AMEN.

I, **Scolds** of **Pryor, Montana** being of sound mind, memory, and understanding, do hereby make and publish this my last will and testament, hereby revoking and annulling all wills by me heretofore made, in manner and form following, that is to say:

First: I direct that all of my just debts and funeral expenses, and expenses of my last illness shall be paid by my executor hereinafter names as soon after my decease as convenient.

Mary Gardner my wife my original allotment bond all the inherited land I have or am heir too. Also I give to Mary Gardner my wife one white horse 6 years old, one bay horse 5 yrs. old branded 6-D one lumber wagon and set of work harness.

To Enos Pretty Horse I give one saddle horse sorrel 8 years old. I also give to Enos Pretty Horse a walking plow 3 horse evener and a drag harrow.

Enos Pretty Horse has 10 head of horses on the range with my brand 6-D on that I want to go to him.

Third: All the rest and residue of my estate, both real and personal and mixed, I give, devise, and bequeath to my lawful heirs as determined after my decease.

And lastly, I do nominate, constitute and appoint **Supt. at Crow Agency, Montana.** executor of this my last will and testament at **Pryor** , Montana, this **20**[th] day of **January** in the year of our Lord one thousand nine hundred and **Twenty**

His

Scolds

Mark.

Signed, sealed, published, and declared by said **Scolds** in our presence, as and for **his** last will and testament, and at **his** request and in our presence and in the presence of each other, we have hereunto subscribed our names as attesting witnesses thereto.

W. P. Marshall	of	**Pryor, Mont.**
Farmer.		
Chas. Bellrock	of	**Pryor, Mont.**
Laborer.		
F. W. Gardner	of	**Pryor, Mont.**
Police.		

19812-21
M H W

DEPARTMENT OF THE INTERIOR
Office of Indian Affairs   MAR 26 1921

It is hereby recommended that the within will of Scolds, deceased allottee No. 542, of the Crow tribe of Indians, in the State of Montana, be approved in accordance with the provisions of the Act of June 25, 1910 (36 Stat. L. 855-6), as amended by Act of February 14, 1913 (37 Stat. L. 678), and the Regulations of the Department.

> Respectfully,
> *E. B. Meritt*
> Assistant Commissioner.

DEPARTMENT OF THE INTERIOR
Office of the Secretary   MAR 30 1921

The within will of Scolds, deceased allottee No. 542, of the Crow tribe of Indians, in the State of Montana, is hereby approved in accordance with the provisions of the Act of June 25, 1910 (36 Stat. L. 855-6), as amended by the Act of February 14, 1913 (37 Stat. L. 678), and the Regulations of the Department.

> *SG Hopkins*
> Assistant Secretary

▲▼▲▼▲▼▲▼▲▼▲▼▲▼

OFFICE OF INDIAN AFFAIRS
RECEIVED
JUL 31 1920
642085

THOMAS CHUCK

I, *Thomas Chuck* being of full age and of sound and deposing mind and memory do declare this to be my last will and testament.

1st. I direct that all my just debts be paid.

2nd. I will and bequeath all my property of which I may die be seized as follows:

Funds on deposit under the supervision of the Superintendent of the Sac & Fox Sanatorium, Toledo, Iowa, as individual Indian money *to my mother Qua-che-wa and all interests which I may have in the Estate of Jim Scott, deceased, which estate is on the Sac & Fox reservation in Oklahoma. Also all personal property.*

I hereby nominate the Superintendent of the Sac & Fox Sanatorium to be executor without bond to this my last will and testament this *13ᵗʰ* day of April, 1920.

> *Thomas Chuck*

Witness:

We hereby certify that on this *13th* day of April, 1920, at the Sac & Fox Reservation, in Tama County, Iowa, *Thomas Chuck* to us personally known did in our presence made the foregoing instrument and declare the same to be his last will and testament and we at his request and in his presence and in the presence of each other do subscribe our names as witnesses thereto.

Jacob Breid
Robert Lyon

DEPARTMENT OF THE INTERIOR
Office of Indian Affairs   MAR 7 1921

The within will of Thomas Chuck, deceased unallotted Sac & Fox Indian, is hereby recommended for approval under the Act of June 25, 1910 (36 Stat. L. 855-6), as amended by Act of February 14, 1913 (37 Stat. L. 678).

E. B. Meritt
Assistant Commissioner.

DEPARTMENT OF THE INTERIOR
Office of the Secretary   MAR 11 1921

The within will of Thomas Chuck, a deceased unallotted Sac & Fox Indian is hereby approved under the Act of June 25, 1910 (36 Stat. L. 855-6), as amended by the Act of February 14, 1913 (37 Stat. L. 678).

SG Hopkins
Assistant Secretary

MOO-TOO

IN THE NAME OF GOD, AMEN : I Moo-Too, Age 86, An Indian of The Nez Perce Indian Reservation, Idaho, now residing at Stites, Idaho. being of sound mind and disposing memory, and not acting under duress, menace or fraud, or undue influence, of any person whatsoever, do hereby make, publish and declare this my LAST WILL AND TESTAMENT, in the manner following, that is to say:

Indian Wills, 1911 – 1921 Book 1
Records of The Bureau of Indian Affairs

First: I direct my body be decently buried with proper regard to my station in life, and the circumstances of my estate.

Second: I direct that my funeral expenses and expenses of my last illness be paid from any funds belonging to my estate, or in the custody of The Superintendant(sic), of the Nez Perce Indian Reservation, Lapwai, Idaho.

Third: I will and bequeath to My daughter Lizzie Stephens, the following discribed(sic) real estate to wit: The south east quarter of The north east quarter, Sec. 4, Twp. 31 N Range 3 E Boise Meridian. containing 40 acres.

To my daughter Julia Morris, The following dicribed(sic) real estate to-wit: North east quarter of the Southwest quarter, Sec-10 Twp. 32 N Range 4 E, Boise, meridian, containing 40 acres more or less.

To my daughter Phoebe Lawrence, the following discribed(sic) real estate to-wit: Lot number one, ~~of~~ and the south east quarter, of the north west quarter of Sec. Number 10 Twp. 32 N Range 4 E, Boise Meridian containing 65.67 acres more or less.

Fourth, Any funds or other personal property I may have at my death shall be shared equaly(sic) by the above names Lizzie Stephens, Julia Morris, And Phoebe Lawrence.

IN WITNESS WHERE OF: I have hereunto put my hand and set my seal this the 19th Day of March A.D. 1917.

her
MOO-TOO (thumb print)
mark

The foregoing instrument was on the date hereof signed, sealed published and declared by said Moo-Too, to be her LAST WILL AND TESTAMENT in the presence of us and at her request and in her presence and in the presence of each other We have subscribed our names as witnesses on this the 19th day of March, A.D. 1917.

Witnessed

John H Rodgers ---------Gov't Farmer
P.O. *Kooskia Idaho*
Almetia Stephens -------House keeper
P.O. *Stites, Idaho*
Ivy Lawrence ------------House keeper
P.O. *Kooskia Idaho*

Probate-67990-13
  JGMcG

DEPARTMENT OF THE INTERIOR
Office of Indian Affairs   OCT –9 1917

It is respectfully recommended that the within will of Moo-too, Nez Perce allottee No. 1655, be approved in accordance with the provisions of the Act of June 25, 1910 (36 Stat. L. 855-6), as amended by the Act of February 14, 1913 (37 Stat. L. 678).

E. B. Meritt
Assistant Commissioner.

DEPARTMENT OF THE INTERIOR
Office of the Secretary   OCT 10 1917

The within will of Moo-too, Nez Perce allottee No. 1655, is hereby approved, in accordance with the provisions of the Act of June 25, 1910 (36 Stat. L. 855-6), as amended by the Act of February 14, 1913 (37 Stat. L. 678).

SG Hopkins
Assistant Secretary

▲▼▲▼▲▼▲▼▲▼▲▼▲▼▲

<u>FEATHER IN HEAD</u>

LAST WILL AND TESTAMENT

OFFICE OF INDIAN AFFAIRS
RECEIVED
AUG -5 1913
95435

I, Feather in Head, of sound mind and disposing memory, do make, declare and publish this my last will and testament whereby revoking and annulling any and all other wills heretofore made by me.

First: It is my will and desire that the expense of my last illness and funeral be paid.

OFFICE OF INDIAN AFFAIRS
RECEIVED
MAR 25 1921
24029

Second:- That all my just debts be paid.

Third:- I do hereby bequeath, will and devise to Spotted Horn, a Grosventres Indian of the Fort Berthold Indian Reservation, who is known by the name of Goes Every Where, and is carried by that name on the rolls of the agency, all of my right, title and interest in and to the allotment of land described as follows: The east one half of the Southeast one quarter of Section six, Twp: 149 North of Range 91 West of the Fifth Principal Meridian and containing 80 acres.

Fourth:- I do hereby bequeath, will and devise to Nora Smith, who is now known by the name of Nora Good Bear, a Grosventres Indian of the Fort Berthold Indian Reservation, and who is my grand-daughter, the South east one quarter of Section one, and the North one half of the North East one quarter of Sec. 13, all in Twp. 149 North of Range 90 West of the Fifth Principal Meridian and containing 240 acres.

Fifth:- I do hereby bequeath, will and devise all other property, both real and personal, or which I may dies possessed, to my son, Goes Every Where, or Spotted Horn, and Nora Smith, also known by the name of Nora Good Bear, each to share equal.

Sixth:- While I have other relations who would likely inherit my land I desire that no other persons or person shall have any part of(sic) portion of my estate, except as hereinbefore mentioned. My other relatives have property enough of their own and are in no need of help from me.

Seventh:-- I do hereby constitute and appoint James Baker, of the Fort Berthold Indian Reservation, Elbowoods, N. D., the executor of this my last will and testament and do hereby request that he act as such.

In witness whereof, I have hereunto published and declared the foregoing instrument to be my last will and testament, at Elbowoods, N. D. on this 31st day of July, 1913, and have hereunto signed myname(sic) as evidence thereof.

Feather in Head, her mark: (thumb print)

On this 31st day of July, 1913, Elbowoods, North Dakota , we, the undersigned persons, were requested to sign the foregoing instrument as witnesses to the will of Feather in Head, by the said Feather in Head making such request and he at the same time declaring it to be his last will and testament and publishing it as such, he signing his name in our presence and we subscribing thereto in the presence of each other.

Name *Jerome Good Bear*
Age *34 yrs old*
Residence *Elbowoods, N.D.*

Indian Wills, 1911 – 1921 Book 1
Records of The Bureau of Indian Affairs

Name *James Baker*
Age *33 yr old*
Residence *Elbowoods, N.D.*

DEPARTMENT OF THE INTERIOR
Office of Indian Affairs   FEB –9 1914
Washington, D. C.

It is recommended that the within will be approved pursuant to the provisions of the Act of June 25, 1910 (36 Stat. L. 855-6), as amended by the Act of February 14, 1913 (37 Stat. L. 678).

Respectfully,
E. B. Meritt
Assistant Commissioner.

DEPARTMENT OF THE INTERIOR
Washington, D. C.   FEB –9 1914

The within will is hereby approved pursuant to the provisions of the Act of June 25, 1910 (36 Stat. L. 855-6), as amended by the Act of February 14, 1913 (37 Stat. L. 678).

SG Hopkins
Assistant Secretary

▲▼▲▼▲▼▲▼▲▼▲▼▲▼▲▼

SHORT WOMAN

Cut Meat, S. D.
March 9 / 1911

Know all men by these presents: --------

That I, Short Woman, do make my last will and testament,

When I die, the whole of my estate is to be turned over to Standing Cloud my only living son.

Short Woman   her
(thumb print)
Witnesses -----   mark
W. B. Gardner
Clinton Black Crow

109

Indian Wills, 1911 – 1921 Book 1
Records of The Bureau of Indian Affairs

DEPARTMENT OF THE INTERIOR

Office of Indian Affairs

It is hereby recommended that the within will be disapproved, under the provisions of the Act of June 25, 1910 (36 Stat. L. 855-6), as amended by the Act of February 14, 1913 (37 Stat. L. 678).

E. B. Meritt
Assistant Commissioner.

DEPARTMENT OF THE INTERIOR

Office of the Secretary   MAR 10 1921

The within will is hereby disapproved under the provisions of the Act of June 25, 1910 (36 Stat. L. 855-6), as amended by the Act of February 14, 1913 (37 Stat. L. 678).

SG Hopkins
Assistant Secretary

▲▼▲▼▲▼▲▼▲▼▲▼▲▼▲▼

MEDICINE MOTHER or MRS. ENEMY HEART

LAST WILL AND TESTAMENT
MEDICINE MOTHER or MRS. ENEMY HEART

I, Medicine Mother or Mrs. Enemy Heart, 66 years of age, a resident of the Fort Berthold Reservation, North Dakota, and an Indian of the Arickara Tribe, being of sound mind and disposing memory do make, declare and publish this as my last will and testament, hereby revoking and annulling all other wills heretofore made by me.

1st. It is my will that my just debts and the expenses incurred in my last sickness and funeral be paid.

2nd. I do hereby will and bequeath and devise unto May Winans, daughter of my adopted daughter, Annie Enemy Heart, all my right, title and interest in and to the NE1/4 SE1/4 of Sec. 32, T. 147 N., R. 89, and the N1/2 of the S1/2 of Sec. 33, T. 147, N., R 89, containing two hundred acres. May Winans is nine years old.

3rd. I do hereby will and bequeath and devise unto Alvin Winans, son of my adopted daughter, Annie Enemy Heart, who is 11 years of age, all my right, title and interest in and to the SE1/4 SE1/4, Sec. 32, and the S1/2 of Sec. 33, all in Twp. 147 N., R. 89, containing Two Hundred acres.

Medicine Mother of
Mrs. Enemy Heart.

Witness to Mark;

Chas D. Ross
Albert H Simpson

On this *19* day of July, A. D. 1918, at *Elbowoods*, N. D., we the undersigned, Charles Ross and Albert Simpson, were requested to sign the foregoing instrument as witnesses to the will of Medicine Mother or Mrs. Enemy Heart by the said Medicine Mother or Mrs. Enemy Heart, making such request and she at the same time, declaring it to be her last will and testament, and publishing it as such, and signing her name in our presence, and we subscribing thereto, each for himself, in her presence, and in the presence of each other.

Chas D. Ross
Albert H Simpson

Probate
14582-21
 M H W
Approval of will
 Mrs. Enemy Heart

DEPARTMENT OF THE INTERIOR
Office of Indian Affairs   MAR 11 1921

The within will of Medicine Mother or Mrs. Enemy Heart, deceased Fort Berthold Indian, is hereby recommended for approval under the Act of June 25, 1910 (36 Stat. L. 855-6), as amended by the Act of February 14, 1913 (37 Stat. L. 678).

E. B. Meritt
Assistant Commissioner.

DEPARTMENT OF THE INTERIOR
Office of the Secretary   MAR 12 1921

The within will of Medicine Mother or Mrs. Enemy Heart, deceased Fort Berthold Indian, is hereby approved under the Act of June 25, 1910 (36 Stat. L. 855-6), as amended by the Act of February 14, 1913 (37 Stat. L. 678).

SG Hopkins
Assistant Secretary

▲▼▲▼▲▼▲▼▲▼▲▼▲▼▲▼

<u>**ZIZIWIN (ZIZI) or MRS. IRON BULL**</u>

In the Name of God, Amen.

I, **Ziziwin** of **Cherry Creek** *in the County of* **Ziebach** , *State of* **South Dakota**, *being of sound mind and memory, and considering the uncertainty of this frail and transitory life, do therefore make, ordain, publish and declare this to be my last Will and Testament:*

FIRST, I order and direct that my Executer hereinafter named, pay all my just debts and funeral expenses as soon after my decease as conveniently may be.

SECOND. After the payment of such funeral expenses and debts, I give, devise and bequeath **unto my grand-son, George Little Crow, all my property, real and personal, in being and in expectancy. My said grand-son, George Little Crow, to inherit all my real estate, that may be mine at the time of my death, either under patent in fee orpatent(sic) in trust, it being my intention hereby to remunerate him for his kindness and love to me in as much as he alone, of all my heirs, has cared and provided for me in my declining years.**

LASTLY, I make, constitute and appoint **F. C. Campbell, Superintendent of the Cheyenne River Indian Reservation, or his regularly qualified and acting successor in office** - - - - - - *to be Executor of this my last Will and Testament, hereby revoking all former wills by me made.*

IN WITNESS WHEREOF, I have hereunto subscribed my name and affixed my seal, the **23rd** *day* of **April** *in the year of our Lord, one thousand nine hundred* **seventeen.**

her thumb

ZIZIWIN   *Seal*

mark.

This Instrument was on the day of the date thereof, signed, published and declared by the said testator **ZIZIWIN** *to be her last Will and Testament in the presence of us who at her request have subscribed our names thereto as witnesses in her presence and in the presence of each other.*

Frank Council Bear
James Bear Stops

Indian Wills, 1911 – 1921 Book 1
Records of The Bureau of Indian Affairs

State of South Dakota)

) ss.

County of Meade)

I, James Bear Stops, being first duly sworn, upon oath, depose and say; that I carefully read the within Last Will and Testament, and that I correctly translated the same into the Sioux language for the understanding of the Testator, Ziziwin, and that she fully understood the contents thereof, before she made her thumb mark in lieu of her signature thereon. That she signed the same in my presence. That I have no interest in the matter what so ever.

James Bear Stops

Subscribed and sworn to before me this 23rd day of April, 1917.

Chas H Zeman
Notary Public in and for
Meade County, South Dakota.

Probate
(56448-19)
 V L D

DEPARTMENT OF THE INTERIOR
Office of Indian Affairs   MAR 7 1921

It is hereby recommended that the within will of Mrs. Iron Bull or Zizi, deceased Cheyenne River Sioux allottee No. 1635, be approved in accordance with the Act of June 25, 1910 (36 Stat. L. 855-6), as amended by the Act of February 14, 1913 (37 Stat. L. 678), and the Regulations of the Department.

Respectfully,
E. B. Meritt
Assistant Commissioner.

DEPARTMENT OF THE INTERIOR
Office of the Secretary   MAR 12 1921

The within will of Mrs. Iron Bull or Zizi or Ziziwin, deceased Cheyenne River Sioux allottee No. 1635, is hereby approved in accordance with the Act of June 25, 1910 (36 Stat. L. 855-6), as amended by the Act of February 14, 1913 (37 Stat. L. 678), , and the Regulations of the Department.

SG Hopkins
Assistant Secretary

▲▼▲▼▲▼▲▼▲▼▲▼▲▼▲▼

SUSAN HILL or QUINCHAS

DEPARTMENT OF THE INTERIOR
UNITED STATES INDIAN SERVICE

I, Susan Hill, whose Indian Name is "Quinchas", declare that I am a female, 64 years of age and am now of sound mind and memory.

I reside at Ignacio, LaPlata County and State of Colorado, am a full blood Ute Indian and belong to the Southern Ute Tribe.

I further declare that I have no living relatives to my knowledge. I live with **Charles Adams**, a Ute Indian and as he is very kind to me and takes care of me in my old age and sickness, I intend to live with him the balance of my life and am under many obligations to him.

Being of sound mind and memory, I make this, my last Will and Testament.

I devise and bequeath to the said **Charles Adams** the following described Real estate, situated in the County of LaPlata and State of Colorado, to-wit:-The North West (NW1/4) quarter of the North West (NW1/4) quarter of Section Eight (8), in Township Thirty Three (33) North of Range Sever (7) West, N.M.P.M.

Also all my personal property of whatsoever nature or kind.

In witness whereof I have hereunto set my hand by making my right thumb mark in the presence of the subscribing witnesses on this 4th. day of September, 1916.

Susan Hill	her thumb mark

Made her thumb mark in our presence and of her own free will and accord

Frank A Hutto Farmer

Martha Morris Field Matron
Ignacio, Colorado.

DEPARTMENT OF THE INTERIOR
Office of Indian Affairs   MAR 8 1921

The within will of Susan Hill or Quinchas, deceased Southern Ute allottee #2 is hereby recommended for approval.

Respectfully,
E. B. Meritt
Assistant Commissioner.

DEPARTMENT OF THE INTERIOR
Office of the Secretary   MAR –9 1921

The within will of Susan Hill or Quinchas, deceased Southern Ute allottee #2 is hereby approved.

SG Hopkins
Assistant Secretary

▲▼▲▼▲▼▲▼▲▼▲▼▲▼▲

<u>HENRY MILTON</u>

𝕿𝖍𝖊 𝕷𝖆𝖘𝖙 𝖂𝖎𝖑𝖑 𝖆𝖓𝖉 𝕿𝖊𝖘𝖙𝖆𝖒𝖊𝖓𝖙

OFFICE OF INDIAN AFFAIRS
RECEIVED
JUN 4- 1919
48183

𝕴𝖓 𝖙𝖍𝖊 𝕹𝖆𝖒𝖊 𝖔𝖋 𝕲𝖔𝖉, 𝕬𝖒𝖊𝖓. 𝕴,

State

Henry Milton *of the ....of* **Phoenix** *County of* **Maricopa** ,   *of Arizona, being of sound and disposing mind and memory, do make, publish and declare this my last WILL AND TESTAMENT, hereby revoking and making null and void all other last Wills and Testaments by me made heretofore.*

𝖅𝖎𝖗𝖘𝖙 – *My Will is that all my just debts and funeral expenses shall be paid out of my Estate, as soon after my decease as shall be found convenient.*

𝕾𝖊𝖈𝖔𝖓𝖉 – *I give, devise and bequeath to* **my daughter Ethel Milton all my lands in the state of Nebraska, which I understand to be the Southwest Quarter and Northeast quarter of Northwest quarter Section twenty three township Twenty four North of Range Nine, and undivided one half interest in Emily Milton allotment, being Southeast Quarter Section Twenty three, Township twenty four North Range eight, all east of the Sixth Principal meridian, Nebraska.**

Third. I give, devise and bequeath to my daughter Ethel, any and all moneys which may be mine after payment of my funeral expenses and other just debts has been made.

Fourth. My Arizona home of 2½ acres near Phoenix, I give devise and bequeath in equal shares to my Daughter Ethel Milton, to Mary Merrick and to Marguerite Merrick, the latter two being my stepdaughters.

*In Testimony Whereof, I have set my hand to this, my Last Will and Testament, at **Phoenix, Arizona** this twelfth day of April in the year of our Lord, One Thousand Nine Hundred **Nineteen (1919)***

*x **Henry Milton***

*The foregoing Instrument was signed by the said **Henry Milton** in our presence and by **him** published and declared as and for **his** Last Will and Testament, and at **his** request, and in **our** presence, and in the presence of*

*each other, we hereunto subscribe our Names as Attesting Witnesses, at **Phoenix, Ariz** this 12 day of April 1919.*

Jno B Brown
*Resides at **Indian School, Phoenix Ariz***

Frances LaChapa
*Resides at **Indian School, Phoenix, Arizona***

Probate
10511--21
 J W H

DEPARTMENT OF THE INTERIOR
Office of Indian Affairs   MAR 3 1921

The within will of Henry Milton, deceased Omaha allottee #230-0, is respectfully recommended for approval under the Act of June 25, 1910 (36 Stat. L. 855-6), as amended by the Act of February 14, 1913 (37 Stat. L. 678).

Respectfully,
E. B. Meritt
Assistant Commissioner.

DEPARTMENT OF THE INTERIOR
Office of the Secretary   MAR 9 1921

Indian Wills, 1911 – 1921 Book 1
Records of The Bureau of Indian Affairs

The within will of Henry Milton, deceased Omaha allottee #230-0, is hereby approved under the Act of June 25, 1910 (36 Stat. L. 855-6), as amended by the Act of February 14, 1913 (37 Stat. L. 678), and the regulations of the Department.

SG Hopkins
Assistant Secretary

FRANK LESSERT

LAST WILL AND TESTAMENT OF FRANK LESSERT
OSAGE ALLOTTEE NO. 1443

I, Frank Lessert, Osage Allottee No. 1443, of Ponca City, State of Oklahoma, being now in good health, strength of body and mind, but sensible of the uncertainty of life, and desiring to make disposition of my property and affairs while in health and strength, do hereby make, publish and declare the following to be my last will and testament, hereby revoking and canceling any and all other or former wills by me at any time made.

(1)   I direct the payment of all my just debts and funeral expenses.

(2)   I give and devise unto my wife, Susan Lessert, the following property, to wit: The Northwest quarter of Section Three (3) Township Twenty-five (25) Range Four (4), East of I.M. in Osage County, State of Oklahoma.

(3)   I direct the payment of One Dollar to each of my children, if living, at the time of my decease.

(4)   I give, devise and bequeath all the rest, residue and remainder of my estate whether real, personal, or mixed to my wife, Susan Lessert.

I hereby appoint and designate my wife, Susan Lessert, sole executrix, without bond, of this my last will and testament.

In witness whereof I, Frank Lessert, Osage Allottee No. 1443, have to this my last will and testament consisting of one sheet of paper, subscribed my name this *11* day of *August* 1914.

Frank H Lessert

Witnesses:

N C Sharp
ES Shidler
Martha Smith

Subscribed by Frank Lessert in the presence of each of us, the undersigned, and at the same time declared by him to us to be his last will and testament, and we thereupon in the presence of Frank Lessert and at his request and in the presence of each other, sign our names hereto as witnesses this *11* day of *August* 1914.

<table>
<tr><td>MISCELLANEOUS
RECEIVED
DEC 29 1920
NO 27687
OSAGE AGENCY</td></tr>
</table>

N C. Sharp
ES Shidler
Martha Smith

We, the undersigned, heirs of Frank Lessert, Sr. deceased, state that Frank Lessert, Sr. died on December 5-1920, and that we have heard read to us a will filed with the Superintendent of the Osage Agency at Pawhuska, Oklahoma, said will dated the 11th day of August 1914, and witnessed by N. C. Sharp, E. S. Shidler and Martha Smith the substance of said will being that the widow Susan Lessert is the sole heir and is named as Executrix without bond, and we have no objection to said will and want it approved.

Signed this 20th day of December, 1920.

Charles Lessert
Walter Lessert
Benjamin(?) Lessert
Frank Lessert, Jr.
Joseph Lessert

DEPARTMENT OF THE INTERIOR
Office of Indian Affairs   MAR -2 1921
The within instrument bearing date of August 11, 1914, purporting to be the last will and testament of Frank Lessert, deceased Osage allottee No. 1443 is hereby recommended for approval under the Act of April 18, 1912, and the regulations of the Department.

Respectfully,
E. B. Meritt
Assistant Commissioner.

DEPARTMENT OF THE INTERIOR
Office of Indian Affairs.   MAR -2 1921

The within instrument bearing date of August 11, 1914, purporting to be the last will and testament of Frank Lessert, deceased Osage allottee No. 1443 is hereby approved under the Act of April 18, 1912, and the regulations of the Department.

SG Hopkins
Assistant Secretary

▲▼▲▼▲▼▲▼▲▼▲▼▲▼▲▼

PHILIP IRON CLOUD

LAST WILL AND TESTAMENT
_______________ of _______________

IN THE NAME OF GOD, AMEN.

I-   *Philip Iron Cloud* being of sound mind, memory and understanding, do hereby make and publish this my last will and testament, hereby revoking and annulling all wills by me heretofore made, in manner and form following that is to say.

First I direct that all my just debts and funeral expenses, and expenses of my last illness shall be paid by my executor hereinafter named as soon after my decease as convenient.

Secon(sic): I give, devise and bequeath to *Samuel Red Bird the SW1/4 of Section 28, Twp. 18, N R. 28, and to Mrs. Alma Codotle I give the NW1/4 of Sect. 28, Twp 18 N. R. 28 all east of the B.H. & M. I also give to Marguerett Iron Cloud, Jasper Iron Cloud & William Red Bird my War risk Insurance, No 3304880 to be divided equally and to each a like.*

Third: All the rest and residue of my estate, both real and personal and mixed I give devise and bequeath to my lawful heirs as detirmened(sic) after my decease

And I do hereby nominate constitute and appoint – *Supt. James B Kitch* or his successor(sic) executor of this my last will and testement(sic).

In Testimony Whereof I have set my hand and seal to this, my last will and testement(sic) at *Wakpala, S.D.* this *12* day of *March* in the year of our Lord one thousand, nine hundred and twenty.

And lastly I hereby request 〜〜 to sign my name to this my last will and testement(sic) and witness the same,

Philip Iron Cloud
Testator or Testrix

Signed, sealed, published and declared by said *Philip Iron Cloud* in our presence, as and for *his* last will and testement(sic) and at *his* request and in our presence and in the presence of each other, we have hereunto subscribed our names as attesting witness thereto.

Forrest F Bliss of *Wakpala S D*
P. J. Deloria of *Wakpala, S.D.*
John Dishihile of *Wakpala, S.D.*

Subscribed and sworn to before a notary Public at Wakpala S.D. this the 12 day of March, 1920.

Floss Godfrey Notary Public
Comm Exp. Jan 17-1922

DEPARTMENT OF THE INTERIOR
UNITED STATES INDIAN SERVICE
WASHINGTON   FEB 15 1921

It is respectfully recommended that the within will of Philip Ironcloud, deceased Standing Rock Sioux Allottee No. 34, be approved under the Act of June 25, 1910 (36 Stats. L., 355), as amended by Act of February 14, 1913 (37 Stats. L. 678).

E. B. Meritt
Assistant Commissioner.

DEPARTMENT OF THE INTERIOR
Office of the Secretary.
WASHINGTON   FEB 21 1921

The within will of Philip Ironcloud, deceased Standing Rock Sioux Allottee No. 34, is hereby approved under the Act of June 25, 1910 (36 Stats. L., 355), as amended by Act of February 14, 1913 (37 Stats. L. 678).

SG Hopkins
Assistant Secretary

JANE MERRICK TURNER

THE LAST WILL AND TESTAMENT
Of
JANE MERRICK TURNER

I, Jane Merrick Turner, of Thurston County, Nebraska, being of sound and disposing mind and memory, and in failing health, do hereby and by these presents make and publish the following as my last will and testament, hereby revoking any former will by me made.

1st. I direct that all my just debts, funeral expenses and the expenses of my last sickness be paid from any funds that I may have on deposit in the Government Office and under the control of the Department of the Interior after my death as the proceeds of the sale of land which I am (unable to read the rest of sentence.)

2nd. I give, devise and bequeath to my three children, Arthur Solomon, Philip Enoch Solomon and Raymond Solomon *share & share equally* all of the money, funds and credits which may belong to me at the time of my death, after the conditions of the first paragraph of this will have been satisfied, or which may be placed to the credit of my estate after my death as the proceeds of the sale (unable to read the remainder of the will).

Jennie M Turner

In the presence of
EJ Bost
Laura Stabler

State of Nebraska   )
Thurston County   ) ss.

We, the undersigned, do hereby certify that we have signed the above instrument as subscribing witnesses in the presence of Jane Merrick Turner, and in the presence of each other and at her request; an that said instrument was fully read to said testatrix in English and interpreted to her in Indian and fully explained to said testatrix in our presence, and she understood the same, and said testatrix did thereupon sign the same.

WITNESS out hands this 22nd day of November, 1917.

E.J. Bost
Laura Stabler

Probate
10709--21
 J W H

DEPARTMENT OF THE INTERIOR
Office of Indian Affairs   MAR 3 1921

It is hereby recommended that the within will of Jane Merrick Turner, deceased allottee No. 102-N of the Omaha Tribe, be approved in accordance with the provisions of the Act of June 25, 1910 (36 Stat. L. 855-6), as amended by the Act of February 14, 1913 (37 Stat. L. 678).

Respectfully,
E. B. Meritt
Assistant Commissioner.

DEPARTMENT OF THE INTERIOR
Office of the Secretary   MAR 8 1921

The within will of Jane Merrick Turner, deceased allottee No. 102-N of the Omaha Tribe, is hereby approved in accordance with the provisions of the Act of June 25, 1910 (36 Stat. L. 855-6), as amended by the Act of February 14, 1913 (37 Stat. L. 678), and the regulations of the Department.

SG Hopkins
Assistant Secretary

▲▼▲▼▲▼▲▼▲▼▲▼▲▼▲▼

ELLA BROWN DOG OR YUNKAHEWIN

Original   *Fire Still Creek, S. Dak.*
                              April 21 – 1917

To all whom these presents shall come, Greetings.

Indian Wills, 1911 – 1921 Book 1
Records of The Bureau of Indian Affairs

The last will and testament of Ella Brown Dog or Yunkahewin.   I hereby bequeath to my Son in Law, Leon Princeau, the South East quarter of the South west quarter and the Lots 5 and 7 of Sec 21 and the South half of the South half of the South west quarter of Sec 22, in Twp 20 north of Range 23 East of the B.H.M. So. Dak. I also bequeath the North west 1/4 Sec 26 Twp 20 R 23 to Mrs. Bertha High Cat, and the North East 1/4 of Sec 27 Twp 20 R 23 to Mrs. Clara Princeau. I am of sound mind and fully realize this and it has been interpreted for me. I bequeath this to Leon Princeau and his wife Clara Princeau on account of their goodness to both my husband and myself. They having taken care of my husband all during his last illness also have they taken care of me during this my last illness.

Her X Mark
Ella Brown Dog
(thumb print)

Witnesses
His X Mark
    (thumb print)
Louis Elk Nation

His X Mark
(thumb print)
David Seventing
Frank W Tihnk(sic)
Helen P. Tahnk

As I have been notified by the Indian Agent Mr. J. B. Kitch of Fort Yates, No. Dak. That there are other heirs for half of my husbands(sic) estate. I hereby relinquish all right and title to the west 1/2 of Sec27 Twp 20 R 23 and claim as my portion the land described in my will and bequeath it to Leon Princeau as my share as that has always been my home. Providing it shall be proven that said heirs to my husbands(sic) land are entitled to share in the said land. And it is further provided that if said heirs are not entitled to the land then I request it shall be equally divided between my daughters Mrs. Clara Princeau and Mrs. Bertha High Cat.

Witnessed   *Her X Mark*
Frank W Tahnk   (thumb print)
Helen P Tahnk

His Mark   *Ella Brown Dog*
    (ink spot)
Louis Elk Nation

DEPARTMENT OF THE INTERIOR
United States Indian Service,   FEB 10 1921
Washington,

It is respectfully recommended that the accompanying last will and testament of Mrs. Brown Dog or Yunkahewin, and the codicil thereto, be approved under the Act of June 25, 1910 (36 Stat. L. 855-6), as amended by the Act of February 14, 1913 (37 Stat. L. 678).

E. B. Meritt
Assistant Commissioner.

DEPARTMENT OF THE INTERIOR
Office of the Secretary,   FEB 28 1921
Washington,

The accompanying will of Mrs. Brown Dog or Hunkahewin(sic), with the codicil thereto, is hereby approved under the Act of June 25, 1910 (36 Stat. L. 855-6), as amended by the Act of February 14, 1913 (37 Stat. L. 678).

SG Hopkins
Assistant Secretary

▲▼▲▼▲▼▲▼▲▼▲▼▲▼▲▼

CINDA (CHARLEY) SWITCH

<u>W I L L</u>
of   CINDA SWITCH.

I, Cinda Switch, of Shawnee, ~~Oklah~~ State of Oklahoma, being of sound mind, and sensible of the uncertainties of life, and desiring to make this disposition of my property and affairs while in sound mind; do hereby publish and declare the following to be my last will and testament, hereby revoking and canceling all other or former wills by me at any time made:

I give and devise to my daughter, Mary Wiley, who is now about, seventeen (17) years of age, and in attendance at the Haskell Indian School, the following described to(sic) to-wit: The East Thirty (30) Acres, of the North half (1/2) of the South East Quarter (1/4) of Section Thirty-three (33), Township Ten (10) North, Range Four (4) East of the Indian Meridian, located in Pottawatomie County, State of Oklahoma.

The balance of my land being Fifty (50) acres, more or less, the remaining part of the North half (1/2) of the South East Quarter (1/4) of Section thirty-three (33) Township Ten (10), North, Range Four (4) East of the Indian Meridian, above described; I give and bequeath to be divided equally between my three (3) sons; Milton Switch, now about eight years of age; Albert Switch, now about five years of age; and Alford Switch, about two years of age.

My daughter, Ruth Cherokee, is omitted from this will; that is she is not to receive any part or consideration herefrom. This arrangement on my part is made for the reason that although Ruth Cherokee is my oldest daughter, she does not take an interest in me as her mother, and has not assisted me in any way during my troubles and hard times, nor has she visited me, and does not even claim to be my daughter.

IN WITNESS WHEREOF, I have to this, my last will and testament, subscribed my name before the witnesses present, this 9th day of February, A. D. 1915.

Her
(thumb print)
Mark.

WITNESSES TO MARK:
 Fred Perkins
 John E. Smoke

Subscribed to in the presence of each of us undersigned, and in our presence declared by her to us to be her last will and testament, and in her presence and in the presence of each of us, we sign our names hereto, as witnesses this 9th day of February, 1915.

Charles Switch
Fred Perkins
John E. Smoke

DEPARTMENT OF THE INTERIOR
Office of Indian Affairs JUL 26 1915

It is respectfully recommended that the within will be approved pursuant to the provisions of the Act of June 25, 1910 (36 Stat. L. 855-6), as amended by the Act of February 14, 1913 (37 Stat. L. 678).

Respectfully,
E. B. Meritt
Assistant Commissioner.

Indian Wills, 1911 – 1921 Book 1
Records of The Bureau of Indian Affairs

DEPARTMENT OF THE INTERIOR
Office of the Secretary,   AUG –6 1915

The within will of Cinda (Charley) Switch, Absentee Shawnee allottee #72, is hereby approved pursuant to the provisions of the Act of June 25, 1910 (36 Stat. L. 855-6), as amended by the Act of February 14, 1913 (37 Stat. L. 678).

A. A. Jones
First Assistant Secretary

▲▼▲▼▲▼▲▼▲▼▲▼▲▼

CHARLES FRANKLIN GIBBS

made duplicates

14989-20
(mnll)

I, Charles Franklin Gibbs, do hereby give, devise, and bequeath unto Eliza Jane Baldwin, all my right, title and interest in and to all lands and monies now due me or to become due me, from the Government of the United States, by virtue of my enrollment in the Fort Berthold Reservation, United States of America.

I hereby declare this to be my last Will and Testament and the consideration for making same is that said Eliza Jane Baldwin has taken care of me during my illness for the past year and will take care of me until my death and she has also agreed to pay my burial expenses.

Dated at Minneapolis, Minnesota, this 6th day of March A. D. 1912.

Charles Franklin Gibbs

Subscribed and sworn to before me, this 6th day of March A. D. 1912

Fry M. Yanacek
NOTARY PUBLIC, HENNEPIN COUNTY

MY COMMISSION EXPIRES SEPTEMBER 21st, 1915.

THIS INSTRUMENT was, on the day of the date thereof, signed, published and declared by the said Testator Charles Franklin Gibbs, to be his Last Will and Testament in our presence, who, at his request, have subscribed our names thereto as witnesses, in his presence and in the presence of each other.

Indian Wills, 1911 – 1921 Book 1
Records of The Bureau of Indian Affairs

Edwin H Brenna   residing at   *4109 Elliott Ave Mpls Minn.*
Anna Edwin Brenna   residing at   *4109 Elliott Ave Mpls Minn*

Probate 14989-21
56855-19 4197-21
   7623-21
  M H W

DEPARTMENT OF THE INTERIOR
Office of Indian Affairs   JUN 20 1921
The within will of Charles (Franklin) Gibbs, deceased Fort Berthold, allottee 1709 –1033a, is hereby recommended for approval under the Act of June 25, 1910 (36 Stat. L. 855-6), as amended by the Act of February 14, 1913 (37 Stat. L. 678), inso(sic) far as it relates to his original allotment.

> Respectfully,
> *E. B. Meritt*
> Assistant Commissioner.

DEPARTMENT OF THE INTERIOR
Office of the Secretary   JUL 14 1921
The within will of Charles (Franklin) Gibbs, deceased Fort Berthold, allottee, is hereby approved under the Act of June 25, 1910 (36 Stat. L. 855-6), as amended by the Act of February 14, 1913 (37 Stat. L. 678), and the Regulations of the Department, insofar as it relates to his original allotment.

> *F M Goodwin*
> Assistant Secretary

▲▼▲▼▲▼▲▼▲▼▲▼▲▼▲▼

WILLIAM ENGLISH

WILL

I, William English, Otoe Indian Allottee No. 247, of the State of Oklahoma, do hereby make, publish and declare this my last Will and Testament, hereby revoking and canceling(sic) all other or former wills made by me:

First. I direct that all my just debts and funeral expenses be paid as soon after my decease as conveniently can be done.

Second. I give and devise to my wife Katie English, the East half (E/2) of SW/4 of Sec. 5. Twp. 23, Range 2E.I.M, containing eight acres on the Otoe

Reservation, Noble County, Oklahoma, also my inherited interest for the estate of Mae Murray, deceased Iowa allottee in Oklahoma.

Third/(sic) I give and devise to my aunt, Mary A. Joans, my undivided one-sixth interest in the allotment of Hartico, deceased Otoe allottee No. 162. Said land being situated in Pawnee County, Oklahoma.

Fourth. I give and devise to my wife, Katie English, all of the rest residue and remainder of my estate, real, personal and mixed, wheresoever situated, of which I may die seized or possessed or to which I may be entitled at the time of my decease.

Fifth. I give and bequeth(sic) to my remaining heirs not mentioned the sum of One ($1.00) each.

Sixth. I nominate, constitute and appoint the Superintendent of the Otoe Indians, as executor of this my last Will and Testament, and I direct that he shall not be required to give any bond or security for the faithful performance of his duties as such.

IN WITNESS WHEREOF, I have hereunto set my hand this 7th day of July, 1920, in the presence of *Mary V. Ely* and *P. C. Little*, whom I have asked to become attesting witnesses hereto.

William English

The foregoing instrument was subscribed, published and declared by William English as and for his last Will and Testament, in our presence and, in the presence of each of us, and we at the same time at his request, in his presence and in the presence of each other, hereunto subscribe our names and residences as attesting witnesses, this seventh day of July, 1920.

Mary V. Ely	Red Rock, Okla.
PC Little	Red Rock, Okla.

Probate

S Y T
Approval of Will
Pawnee Agency,
Oklahoma

Indian Wills, 1911 – 1921 Book 1
Records of The Bureau of Indian Affairs

DEPARTMENT OF THE INTERIOR
Office of Indian Affairs, Washington
JUN 20 1921

It is recommended that the within will be approved pursuant to the provisions of the Act of June 25, 1910 (36 Stat. L. 855-6), as amended by the Act of February 14, 1913 (37 Stat. L. 678), with the exception of the paragraph appointing an executor.

> Respectfully,
> *E. B. Meritt*
> Assistant Commissioner.

DEPARTMENT OF THE INTERIOR
Office of the Secretary, Washington
JUL 14 1921

The within will is hereby approved pursuant to the provisions of the Act of June 25, 1910 (36 Stat. L. 855-6), as amended by the Act of February 14, 1913 (37 Stat. L. 678), with the exception of the paragraph appointing an executor.

> *F M Goodwin*
> Assistant Secretary

SAMUEL SMILEY

LAST WILL AND TESTAMENT OF SAMUEL SMILEY

CHEYENNE RIVER ALLOTTEE NO. 182

I, Samuel Smiley, Cheyenne River Allottee No. 182 do hereby make and declare this to be my last will and testament.

In the event of my death, all my property of which I may die posessed(sic) is to go to my wife, Nina Smiley, Cheyenne River Allottee No. 2693, including any money that I may have in the bank, and one I.D. buckskin gelding, branded H.H. on the left thigh. In the event that my wife should die before I do then all my property of whatsoever nature that I may die posessed(sic) shall go to my step-daughter, Nellie LeBeau, who has taken care of me for seven years while I have been blind and could not care for myself and who is entitled to consideration for her kindness.

Witness to mark: His
Loren O. Johnson   Samuel Smiley
Luke Gilbert   Allottee No. 182. Thumb print.

We, the undersigned, Loren O. Johnson, and Luke Gilbert, employees of the United States Indian Service at Cheyenne Agency, S. D. hereby declare that his name was written by Loren O. Johnson at the request of Samuel Smiley, that he was of sound mind and disposing memory at the time this will was executed, and that he has stated that he does not wish his money to go to the children of his brothers and sisters in the event that his wife should die before he does but that he makes this will in order to protect the interest of his step-daughter, Nellie LeBeau who has taken care of himself and wife for seven years while he was blind.

Loren O Johnson
Luke Gilbert

Dated and subscribed at Cheyenne Agency, South Dakota on the 12th day of December, A. D., 1916.

L-H
1382-17
V L D
DEPARTMENT OF THE INTERIOR
Office of Indian Affairs, Washington
FEB –3 1917

The within will is hereby recommended for approval, in accordance with the Act of June 25, 1910 (36 Stat. L. 855-6), as amended by the Act of February 14, 1913 (37 Stat. L. 678).

Respectfully,
E. B. Meritt
1-JMM-18   Assistant Commissioner.

DEPARTMENT OF THE INTERIOR
Office of the Secretary, Washington
FEB –9 1917

The within will is hereby approved, in accordance with the provisions of the Act of June 25, 1910 (36 Stat. L. 855-6), as amended by the Act of February 14, 1913 (37 Stat. L. 678).

Bo Sweeney
Assistant Secretary

▲▼▲▼▲▼▲▼▲▼▲▼▲▼▲▼

TE-TAH-PIL-MA

<u>WILL</u>

IN THE NAME OF GOD, AMEN: I, Te-tah-pil-ma, age 79, an Indian of the Nez Perce Reservation, Idaho, now residing at Lapwai, Idaho, being of sound mind and disposing memory, and not acting under duress, menace, fraud, or undue influence, of any person whatsoever, do hereby make, publish, and declare this my LAST WILL AND TESTAMENT, in the manner following, that is to say:

First: I direct that my body be decently buried with proper regard to my station in life, and the circumstances of my estate.

Second: I direct that my funeral expenses and expenses of my last illness be paid from any funds belonging to my estate, or in the custody of the Superintendent of the Nez Perce Indian Reservation, Lapwai, Idaho.

Third: I will and bequeath to Jospehine(sic) Carter Lot 24 of my own allotment on the Nez Perce Reservation, No. 1953, described as Lots, 21, 22, 23, and 24, of Sec. 5, T. 34 N., R 3 W., B: M.

Fourth: I will and bequeath to Lewis Carter Lot 23 of my own allotment as described above.

Fifth: I will and bequeath to Albert Brinkham Lot 22 of my own allotment as described above.

Sixth: I will and bequeath to Rachel Henry Lot 21 of my own allotment as described above.

Seventh: I will and bequeath to Corbett Lawyer that part of allotment No. 198 in-herited from my husband, John Cutnose, remaining unsold.

Eighth: I will and bequeath to Elizabeth Carter and Isaah Carter equal interests in the one-half interest inherited by me in the allotment of Nuse No Po, No. 199.

Ninth: I will and bequeath to my natural heirs to share equally all funds remaining to my credit at the Nez Perce Agency, after payment of my debts and funeral expenses.

In witness thereof I have hereunto put my hand and seal this **26th** day of **November**, 1920.

Her
TE-TAH-PIL-MA (thumb print)
Mark

The foregoing instrument was on the date hereof signed, sealed, published, and declared by said Te-tah-pil-ma to be her LAST WILL AND TESTAMENT, in the presence of us, and at her request and in her presence, and in the presence of each other, we have subscribed our names as witnesses on this **26th** day of **November**, 1920.

> *Frank L Dailey*
> *David McFarland*
> *Sam H. Lipps*

Probate
47363-21
 J W H

DEPARTMENT OF THE INTERIOR
Office of Indian Affairs   JUN 21 1921

The within will of Te tah pil ma, deceased Nez Perce allottee #1953 is hereby recommended for approval, in accordance with the Act of June 25, 1910 (36 Stat. L. 855-6), as amended by the Act of February 14, 1913 (37 Stat. L. 678), and the Regulations of the Department.

> Respectfully,
> *E. B. Meritt*
> Assistant Commissioner.

DEPARTMENT OF THE INTERIOR
Office of the Secretary   JUL 1- 1921

The within will of Te tah pil ma, deceased Nez Perce allottee #1953 is hereby approved, in accordance with the provisions of the Act of June 25, 1910 (36 Stat. L. 855-6), as amended by the Act of February 14, 1913 (37 Stat. L. 678), and the Regulations of the Department.

> *F M Goodwin*
> Assistant Secretary

▲▼▲▼▲▼▲▼▲▼▲▼▲▼▲▼

CHARLES PRIMEAUX

I, Charles Primeaux, Ponca allottee No. 157, age 52 years being now sound in body and mind but conscious of the uncertainty of life desire to make the following disposition of my property:

FIRST I desire that my just debts and funeral expenses be paid.

SECOND I hereby give and bequeath unto my son, Lamont Primeaux age 26 years, that part of my allotment described as the NE/4 of the SE/4, Sec. 10, Twp. 25N, Range 2 East.

THIRD I hereby give and bequeath unto my daughter, Zoie Prineaux age 16 years, that part of my allotment described as the NW/4 of the SE/4 of Sec. 10, Twp. 25N, Range 2 East.

FOURTH If I have a wife at the time of my death unto her I give the sum of $1.00, and a like amount to any near relative who may claim to be an heir.

FIFTH Of all other property of which I may be possessed I give in equal shares to my son and daughter, Lamont Primeaux and Zoie Primeaux. This includes my undivided one third interest in the allotment of my deceased wife, Kate S. B. Primeaux, described as the W/2 of the NW/4, Sec. 23, Twp. 25N, Range 2 East, and (42527-1917) and my undivided 1/21(sic) interest in the allotment of Standing Buffalo, S/2 of the SW/4, Sec. 14, Twp. 25, Range 2 East (84304-1912 and 84311-1912.)

SIXTH This will is make subject to the approval of the Secretary of the Interior.

Done at the Ponca Indian Agency, Whiteagle, Oklahoma, on the 6th day of February 1919, in the presence of John F DeJarnette, Irene Chisholm and Elijah Bayhylle as witnesses.

Charles Primeaux

Witnesses:

John F. DeJarnette
Elijah L. Bayhylle
Irene Chisholm

Probate
14489-19
40114-21
 J M P

DEPARTMENT OF THE INTERIOR
Office of Indian Affairs   JUL 9 1921

The within will of Charles Primeaux, deceased allottee No. 157 of the Ponca Tribe, is hereby recommended for approval, in accordance with the Act of June 25, 1910 (36 Stat. L. 855-6), as amended by the Act of February 14, 1913 (37 Stat. L. 678).

Respectfully,
E. B. Meritt
Assistant Commissioner.

DEPARTMENT OF THE INTERIOR
Office of the Secretary   JUL 14 1921

The within will of Charles Primeaux, deceased allottee No. 157 of the Ponca Tribe, is hereby approved, in accordance with the provisions of the Act of June 25, 1910 (36 Stat. L. 855-6), as amended by the Act of February 14, 1913 (37 Stat. L. 678).

F M Goodwin
Assistant Secretary

▲▼▲▼▲▼▲▼▲▼▲▼▲▼▲▼

<u>**LOUISE HIS DAY**</u>
W I L L

IN THE NAME OF GOD AMEN:

I, **Luise**(sic) **His Day** Fort Peck allottee No. **1377** residing at **Frazier** Montana, being of sound mind but of feeble health and realizing the uncertainty of life, and not acting under fraud, duress, menace or undue influence, do this **28** day of **July** 1920, make publish and declare the following to be my last will and testament.

Indian Wills, 1911 – 1921 Book 1
Records of The Bureau of Indian Affairs

First:

I give, devise and bequeath **to my beloved husband Walter His Day My overlane Car and Irrigatele(sic) 40 The NE L/4 of NE L/4 of section 5, Township 26, N. range 45. E.**

Second:

I give, devise and bequeath **To my beloved Father Growing Four Times the 7 head of Mares and colts, these horses are out on the range branded with my father's brand** ⅀⅃/ **on right Jaw.**

Third:

I give, devise and bequeath **I want my little sister remine(sic) with my grandfather while he is living. And after his death she can go back to her Father Growing Four Times.**

I hereby appoint E. D. Mossman, Supt. of Fort Peck Agency, or his successor in office as executor of my estate.

Louise His Day
Fort Peck allottee No. **1377**

Witnesses:

Isaac Blount
Tessa Blount

We, the undersigned, hereby certify on our honor that neither of us are related in any way to the testat..., that we were both present and witnessed the signature of the testat... to the above instrument in one page which... read and fully understood before signing as ... was apparently of sound mind and signed the same of ... own free will and accord stating that ... wishes were duly set forth.

Isaac Blount Farmer
Tessa Blount

Probate
39409-21
 J M P

DEPARTMENT OF THE INTERIOR
Office of Indian Affairs   JUN 15 1921

The within will of Louise His Day allotted as Louise Growing Four Times, deceased allottee No. 1377 of the Assiniboine tribe, is hereby recommended for approval under the Act of June 25, 1910 (36 Stat. L. 855-6), as amended by the Act of February 14, 1913 (37 Stat. L. 678).

> Respectfully,
> *E. B. Meritt*
> Assistant Commissioner.

DEPARTMENT OF THE INTERIOR
Office of the Secretary   JUN 16 1921

The within will of Louise His Day allotted as Louise Growing Four Times, deceased allottee No. 1377 of the Assiniboine tribe, is hereby approved under the Act of June 25, 1910 (36 Stat. L. 855-6), as amended by the Act of February 14, 1913 (37 Stat. L. 678).

> *F M Goodwin*
> Assistant Secretary

▲▼▲▼▲▼▲▼▲▼▲▼▲▼▲▼

TAMASASAMI

LAST WILL AND TESTAMENT.

IN THE NAME OF GOD, AMEN:

I, **Tamasasami**, of Umatilla Indian Reservation, Oregon, being of sound mind, memory and understanding, do hereby make and publish this my last will and testament, hereby revoking and annulling all wills by me heretofore made, in manner and form following, that is to say:

FIRST: I direct that all my just debts and funeral expenses, and expenses of my last illness, shall be paid as soon after my decease as shall be convenient.

SECOND: I give, devise and bequeath to James Kash and his wife, Julia Kash Kash(sic), in equal shares, 160 acres of land inherited by me from my deceased husband, Tintinmeetsa, Cayuse allottee No. 90, and described as the W/2 of NE/4 and E/2 of NW/4 Sec. 16, T. 2 N, R 34, East of the Williamette Meridian, in Oregon.

IN TESTIMONY WHEREOF, I have set my hand and seal to this, my last will and testament, at my home on the Umatilla Reservation, this **20th** day of

Indian Wills, 1911 – 1921 Book 1
Records of The Bureau of Indian Affairs

April, in the year of our Lord, One Thousand Nine Hundred and **Twenty**.

Tamasasami

Her
(thumb print)
Mark

SIGNED, sealed published and declared by the said **Tamasasami** in our presence, as and for **her** last will and testament, and at **her** request and in our presence, and in the presence of each other, we have hereunto subscribed our names as attesting witnesses thereto.

Allen Patawa
Otis Halfmoon
Amy M Hazen
Umatilla Indian Reservation.
Oregon.

DEPARTMENT OF THE INTERIOR
Office of Indian Affairs   JUN -6 1921

The within will of Tamasasami is hereby recommended for approval in accordance with the Act of June 25, 1910 (36 Stat. L. 855-6), and the Act of February 14, 1913 (37 Stat. L. 678).

Respectfully,
E. B. Meritt
Assistant Commissioner.

DEPARTMENT OF THE INTERIOR
Office of the Secretary   JUN 10 1921

The within will of is hereby approved in accordance with the Act of June 25, 1910 (36 Stat. L. 855-6), and the Act of February 14, 1913 (37 Stat. L. 678).

F M Goodwin
Assistant Secretary

▲▼▲▼▲▼▲▼▲▼▲▼▲▼▲▼

EDNA CHIEF OR EDNA KILLS IN TIMBER

Will.

I, **Edna Kills In Timber** of Pine Ridge Agency, South Dakota, Allottee number **3929** do hereby make and declare this to be my last will and testament, in accordance with Section 2 of the Act of June 24, 1910, (36 stat.

855-858), and Act of February 14, 1913 (Public No. 381), hereby revoking all former wills made by me:

1. I hereby direct that as soon as possible after my decease, that all my debts, funeral and testamentary expenses be paid out of my personal estate.

2. I give and devise my allotment on the Pine Ridge Reservation, South Dakota, described as follows: **S/2 of Section 8 in Township Forth-three north of Range Thirty-five west of the Sixth Principal Meridian in South Dakota, containing 320 acres of land,** in the following manner: **The SW/4 of Section 8 in Township Forty-three north of Range Thirty-five, to my husband, Albert Kills-in-timber; and to my sons, Earl and Garnett Goings, in equal parts. The Se/4 of Section 8 in Township Forty-three north of Range Thirty-five, to Mrs. Rosa Ecoffey, my cousin.**

3. I give and bequeath all of my personal property of whatsoever nature and wheresoever situated unto **my husband, Albert Kills-in-timber.**

4. All the rest of my property, real or personal, now possessed or hereafter acquired, of whatsoever nature and wheresoever situated, I hereby give, devise and bequeath unto **my sons, Earl and Garnett Goings, in equal shares.**

In witness whereof I have hereunto set my hand this **twenty-eight** day of **September, 1918.** 191....

Edna Kills in Timber

The above statement was this 28th day of September, 1918   191... signed and publish by Edna Kills-in-timber as her last will and testament, in the joint presence of the undersigned, the said Edna Kills-in-timber then being of sound and vigorous mind and free from any constraint or compulsion: whereupon we being without any interest in the matter other than friendship, and being well acquainted with her but not members of her family, immediately subscribed our names hereto in the presence of each other and of the said testator for the purpose of attesting the said will as she requested us to do. And that I, at the testa...s(sic) request, have written (left blank) name in ink and that (left blank) affixed (left blank) thumb marks.

<table>
<tr><td></td><td align="right">Post Office Address</td></tr>
<tr><td>George A Trotter</td><td align="right">Pine Ridge, S. D.</td></tr>
<tr><td>Robert H Fulzner</td><td align="right">Pine Ridge, S. D.</td></tr>
</table>

Pine Ridge, South Dakota

September 28, 1918

Pine Ridge Agency,
Pine Ridge, S. Dak.,
April 14, 1921.

I hereby certify that I have fully inquired into the mental competency of the Indian signing the above will, the circumstances attending the execution of the will; the influence that may have induced its execution, and the names of those entitled to share in the estate under the law of descent in South Dakota: reasons for the disposition of the property proposed by the will, differing from disposition had the property descended by operation of law.

I respectfully forward this will with the recommendation that it be ….approved.

H. M. Tidwell
Supt. & Spl. Disb. Agent.

DEPARTMENT OF THE INTERIOR
Office of Indian Affairs   JUN 17 1921

The inclosed(sic) will of Edna Chief or Edna Kills In Timber is hereby recommended for approval in accordance with the Act of June 25, 1910 (36 Stat. L. 855-6), and the Act of February 14, 1913 (37 Stat. L. 678).

Respectfully,
E. B. Meritt
Assistant Commissioner.

DEPARTMENT OF THE INTERIOR
Office of the Secretary   JUN 22 1921

The within will is hereby approved in accordance with the Act of June 25, 1910 (36 Stat. L. 855-6), and the Act of February 14, 1913 (37 Stat. L. 678).

F M Goodwin
Assistant Secretary

LITTLE BIRD

ROSEBUD AGENCY
RECEIVED
MAY 7 1920

OFFICE OF INDIAN AFFAIRS
RECEIVED
Jun 3- 1921
47030

LAST WILL AND TESTAMENT

IN THE NAME OF GOD, AMEN: I *Little Bird* of *Okreek in the County* of *Todd* and State of *So. Dakota* being of sound mind and memory, and considering the uncertainty of this frail and transitory life, do therefore make, ordain, publish and declare this to be my Last Will and Testament.

First, I order and direct that my executor hereinafter named, pay all my just debts and funeral expenses as soon after my decease as conveniently may be.

Second, After the payment of such funeral expenses and debts, I give, devise and bequeath: *Unto my two sisters, Irene or Red Cow, and Ptesan-wastin-in or Mrs. Jennie Black Bonnet and my brother Plenty Horse, share and share alike in the quarter of sec. (blank) Township 39, Range 26 west of the P.M. and the other quarter of my allot. to my husband, White Prairie Dog for him to use as he sees fit.*

Lastly, I make, constitute and appoint the Superintendent of the Rosebud Indian Agency as Executor of this, My Last Will and Testament, hereby revoking all former Wills by me made.

IN TESTIMONY WHEREOF, I have hereunto subscribed my name and affixed my seal, the *26* day of *April*, in the year of Our Lord One Thousand Nine Hundred *twenty*.

her

Little Bird   (thumb print x2)

mark

THIS INSTRUMENT was, on the day of the date thereof, signed, published and declared by the said testat... *Little Bird* to be her Last Will and Testament, in our presence, who, at her request, have subscribed our names thereto as witnesses, in her presence and in the presence of each other.

B P Lambert   Residing at *Okreek, S.D.*

Thomas (Illegible)   Residing at *Okreek, S.D.*

We the above witnesses certify that the two thumb marks were made by her.

her

Little Bird   (thumb print)

Mark

DEPARTMENT OF THE INTERIOR

Office of Indian Affairs   JUN 23 1921

The within will is recommended for approval under the provisions of the Act of June 25, 1910 (36 Stat. L. 855-6), as amended by the Act of February 14, 1913 (37 Stat. L. 678).

Indian Wills, 1911 – 1921 Book 1
Records of The Bureau of Indian Affairs

E. B. Meritt
Assistant Commissioner.

DEPARTMENT OF THE INTERIOR
Office of the Secretary   JUN 29 1921

The within will is hereby approved under the provisions of the Act of June 25, 1910 (36 Stat. L. 855-6), as amended by the Act of February 14, 1913 (37 Stat. L. 678).

F M Goodwin
Assistant Secretary

▲▼▲▼▲▼▲▼▲▼▲▼▲▼▲▼

<u>HIS LAW</u>   *2690 – 21*
                                                               wmll

LAST WILL AND TESTAMENT OF
HIS LAW, CROW CREEK
ALLOTTEE NO. 166.
------oOo------

<u>IN THE NAME OF GOD, AMEN</u>:

I, HIS LAW, 60 yeares of age, an allottee of the Crow Creek reservation, in the state of South Dakota, knowing the shortness and uncertainty of life and having for the past month been confined to my home by illness, desire while I am of sound mind, memory and understanding to make and declare this my last will and testament, hereby revoking and annulling(sic) all wills by me heretofore made, that is to say:

<u>FIRST</u>:   I direct that all my just debts and funeral expenses, and the expenses of my last illness be paid as soon after my decease as will be convenient.

<u>SECOND</u>   I am posessed(sic) of an allotment of land within the boundary of the Crow Creek reservation, in the state of South Dakota, said allotment being described as the SE/4; E/2 of the SW/4 and Lots 3 & 4, Section 19, Twp.107 N., Range 69W., 5th P.M. South Dakota, containing 315.21 acres, the same having been allotted to me under the Act of March 2, 1889 (25 Stat. L., 888), trust patent for same being issued under date of December 12, 1895, a portion of this allotment described as the SE/4 Section 19, Township 107 N, Range 69, 160 acres, having been sold by me during the year 1919, of the remaining portion of

the same, described as the E/2 of the SW/4 and Lots 3 & 4, Sec. 19, Township 107 N., Range 69, 160 acres, having been sold by me during the year 1919, of the remaining portion of the same, described as the E/2 of the SW/4 and Lots 3 & 4 Sec, 19, Twp. 107 N., Range 69 W, 5th P. M. South Dakota, containing 155.21 acres, I give, devise and bequeath to the following names persons, to wit:

To my daughter, Ida His Law, I give all of my above remaining allotment, together with the house in which I am now living also barn, one grey mare, with wagon and harness, I desire that she receive this as she has had a hard time caring for me during my illness and is alone and needs the same more than any of the rest of my children, it is also my belief that she has more than earned what I am able to give her as she has always stayed with me and mad a home for me.

I have about $500.00 derived from the sale of my allotment on deposit in the office of the of the Superintendent of the Crow Creek reservation, of this money it is my desire that my son Joseph His Law, receive $150.00, the remainder I desire to be equally divided between my son Marion His Law, and my daughters Ida and Elizabeth. I am not making further provision for my son Marion His Law and my daughter Elizabeth as they are fully able to care for themselves.

Sheet 2 of the Will of His Law.

AND LASTLY: I am satisfied that the officers in charge of the Department of the Interior of the United States will make proper provision for carrying into effect of this my last will and testament and, therefore, I have not appointed an executor.

IN TESTIMONY WHEREOF, I have set my hand and seal, to this my last will and testament at my home located near the row Creek agency, at Ft. Thompson, South Dakota, on this 31st day of December 1920, and request that Peter W. Lightfoot, Charles McBride and Jesse McBride, all of Fort Thompson, South Dakota, witness my signing of the same and affix their names as attesting witnesses thereto.

His

His Law   (thumb print)

Mark

Indian Wills, 1911 – 1921 Book 1
Records of The Bureau of Indian Affairs

Witnesses

Peter W. Lightfoot
Charles McBride

Signed, sealed, published and declared by the said His Law, in our presence as and for his last will and testament, and at his request and in his presence and in the presence of each other we have hereto subscribed our names as attesting witnesses thereto this 31st day of December 1920.

Peter W Lightfoot
Charles McBride
Jesse McBride

Probate
41748-21
 M H W

DEPARTMENT OF THE INTERIOR
Office of Indian Affairs   JUN 23 1921

It is hereby recommended that with within will of His Law, deceased Crow Creek allottee #166, be approved under the Act of June 25, 1910 (36 Stat. L. 855-6), as amended by the Act of February 14, 1913 (37 Stat. L. 678).

Respectfully,
E. B. Meritt
Assistant Commissioner.

DEPARTMENT OF THE INTERIOR
Office of the Secretary   JUN 27 1921

The within will of His Law, deceased Crow Creek allottee #166, is hereby approved under the Act of June 25, 1910 (36 Stat. L. 855-6), as amended by the Act of February 14, 1913 (37 Stat. L. 678), and the Regulations of the Department.

F M Goodwin
Assistant Secretary

6-22
AD 1921

▲▼▲▼▲▼▲▼▲▼▲▼▲▼▲▼

<u>ANNETTE CATHAWAY</u>

143

Colo Pines Agency
Parker, Ariz
May 8th, 1918

I, Annette Cathaway, being of sound mind and feeling that my illness is hopeless, do hereby make my last will & testament. I do hereby give & bequeath my own individual allotment of 10 acres to my brother Allen Amiely nay, my share the allotments of my deceased children. I desire to go to my little girl Thelma to be cared for & held in trust for her until she becomes of age by her Father.
My reason for leaving my individual allotment t my brother Allen is that I believe my share in the dead children's(sic) allotments will be at least 10 acres & will be as much as the child can manage.

her

Annette Amiely nay X Cathaway
Annette Cathaway

Witnesses
Wilma G Rhodes
Washington D.C. Indian Office

Merritt Laffoon
Parker, Arizona

Probate
10515-21
DEPARTMENT OF THE INTERIOR
Office of Indian Affairs

The within will of Annette A. Cathaway is hereby recommended for approval in accordance with the Act of June 25, 1910 (36 Stat. L. 855-6), as amended by the Act of February 14, 1913 (37 Stat. L. 678).

Respectfully,
E. B. Meritt
Assistant Commissioner.

DEPARTMENT OF THE INTERIOR
Office of the Secretary   JUN 21 1921
The within will is hereby approved in accordance with the Act of June 25, 1910 (36 Stat. L. 855-6), as amended by the Act of February 14, 1913 (37 Stat. L. 678).

Indian Wills, 1911 – 1921 Book 1
Records of The Bureau of Indian Affairs

F M Goodwin
Assistant Secretary

▲▼▲▼▲▼▲▼▲▼▲▼▲**REC'D**

<u>**FANNIE BAD WOUND, nee RED HOOP**</u>

WILL

FEB 4 1918
Pine Ridge Agency,
S. Dak.

I, Fannie Bad Wound, nee Red Hoop of Pine Ridge Agency, South Dakota, Allottee number 5631 do hereby make and declare this to be my last will and testament, in accordance with Section 2 of the Act of June 25, 1910, (36 stat. 855-858), and Act of February 14, 1913, (Public No. 381), hereby revoking all former wills made by us:

1. I hereby direct that as soon as possible after my decease that all my debts funeral and testamentary expenses be paid out of my personal estate.

2. I give and devise my allotment on the Pine Ridge Reservation, South Dakota, described as follows; **No. 5631, The Lots 1 & 2 and S/2 of NE/4 of Sec. 1; T. 41 N., R. 37 W. unto my sister, Maggie or Ophelia Chips.**

My 1/4 section inherited from my father, Red Hoop, Allottee No. 5630, described as Lots 3, 4, & 5 and SE/4 of NW/4 of Sec. 6, T. 41 N., R. 36 W. unto my brother Edward Little Killer.

My undivided half interest in SE/4 of Sec. 6, T. 41 N, R. 36 W, unto my daughter, Clara Viena Bad Wound. And further provided that if my daughter dies before she becomes of age, that this land be given unto my Nephew, Geoffrey Chips.

And my undivided one half interest in my mother, Two Nostrils allotment No. 4355, described as The N/2 of Sec. 16, T. 41 N, R. 34 W, my share of which is 160 acres, unto my daughter, Clara Viena Bad Wound.

And my undivided one half interest in my deceased daughters, Catherine Hazel Bad Wound, described as Lots 3 & 4 and S/2 of NW/4 of Sec. 2 in Twp. 42 N., R. 34 W, Allotment No. 8135; unto my husband Gilbert Bad Wound.

3. I give and bequeath all of my personal property of whatsoever nature and wheresoever situated unto **my brother and sister as follows, to my Brother,**

Edward Little Killer, my hay rake, and to my sister Maggie hips, my wagon, and all other personal property of which I am possessed(sic) of unto my daughter, Clara Viena Bad Wound.

4. All the rest of my property real or personal now possessed or hereafter acquired of whatsoever nature and wheresoever situated, I hereby give, devise and bequeath unto **my daughter, Clara Viena Bad Wound.**

In witness whereof I have hereunto set my hand this **Thirtieth** day of **January, 1918**

Fannie Bad Wound

The above statement was, this **30th** day of **January** 1918 signed and published by **Fannie Bad Wound** as **her** last will and testament in the joint presence of the undersigned, the said **Fannie Bad Wound** then being of sound and vigorous mind and free from any constraint or compulsion: whereupon we being without any interest in the matter other than friendship and being well acquainted with **her** but not members of **her** family, immediately subscribed our names hereto in the presence of each other and of the said testator, for the purpose of attesting the said will as **she** requested us to do.

<table>
<tr><td></td><td>Post Office Address</td></tr>
<tr><td>George Bartlett</td><td>Wanblee, S. D.</td></tr>
<tr><td>(Illegible) Chips</td><td>Wanblee, S. D.</td></tr>
</table>

Pine Ridge, South Dakota

May 24, 1921

I hereby certify that I have fully inquired into the mental competency of the Indian signing the above will; the circumstances attending the execution of the will, the influence that may have induced its execution and the names of those entitled to share in the estate under the law of descent in South Dakota: reasons for the disposition of the property proposed by the will, differing from disposition had the property descended by operation of law.

I respectfully forward this will with the recommendation that it be approved.

H. M. Tidwell
Supt. & Spl. Disb. Agent

▲▼▲▼▲▼▲▼▲▼▲▼▲▼

HIS HORSE LOOKING

LASTWILLANDTESTAMENT
OF
His Horse Looking

IN THE NAME OF GOD, AMEN.

I ***His Horse Looking*** OF ***Little Eagle, SD*** BEING OF SOUND MIND, MEMORY AND UNDERSTANDING, DO HEREBY MAKE AND PUBLISH THIS MY LAST WILL AND TESTAMENT, HEREBY REVOKING AND ANNULLING ALL WILLS BY ME HERETOFORE MADE, IN MANNER AND FORM FOLLOWING THAT IS TO SAY:

FIRST: I DIRECT THAT ALL MY JUST DEBTS AND FUNERAL EXPENSES, AND EXPENSES OF MY LAST ILLNESS SHALL BE PAID BY MY EXECUTOR HEREINAFTER NAMED AS SOON AFTER MY DECEASE AS CONVENIENT;

SECOND: I GIVE, DEVISE AND BEQUEATH TO:

To my grandson, Noah Wakuramani Se 1/2 of S 8, Twp 20, R27,

To my Grand daughter, Eunis(sic) **Wakutamani Se 1/2, of S 12, Twp 20, R26**

To my grand daughter, Agnes Wakutamani Ne 1/2 of S12, Twp 20, R26

To my grand daughter, Eunice Wakutamani, one red cow brand 485 Right (no particular place given)

To Agnes Wakutamani, one red white face cow brand 485 right side,

To Mrs. Half My Sister, one Yearling Heafer(sic)**, white face, Brand 485**

To Agnes Wakutamani, one spoted(sic) **mair**(sic) **brand 485**

Indian Wills, 1911 – 1921 Book 1
Records of The Bureau of Indian Affairs

To Wakutamani, or walking shorter time, one Squaw wagon, one set of harness one spring wagon one bay gelding horse brand 485, one lumber wagon.

THIRD: ALL THE REST AND RESIDUE OF MY ESTATE, BOTH REAL AND PERSONAL AND MIXED, I GIVE, DEVISE AND BEQUEATH TO MY LAWFUL HEIRS DETERMINED AFTER MY DECEASE.

AND, I DO HEREBY NOMINATE, CONSTITUTE AND APPOINT *James B Ketch, Supt of Standing Rock Res* EXECUTOR FOR THIS MY LAST WILL AND TESTAMENT.

IN TESTIMONY WHEREOF, I HAVE SET MY HAND AND SEAL TO THIS, MY LAST WILL AND TESTAMENT, AT *Little Eagle, South Dakota.* THIS *fifth* DAY OF *January* IN THE YEAR OF OUR LORD ONE THOUSAND NINE HUNDRED AND *18*.

AND LASTLY, I HEREBY REQUEST *Robt Holsclaw* TO SIGN MY NAME TO THIS MY LAST WILL AND TESTAMENT AND WITNESS THE SAME.

X his mark (thumb print) *His Horse Looking*
TESTATOR OR TESTATRIX.

SIGNED, SEAL, PUBLISH AND DECLARED BY SAID *His Horse Looking* IN (Unable to read print) ..... IN THE PRESENCE OF EACH OTHER WE HAVE HEREUNTO SUBSCRIBED OUR NAMES AS ATTESTING WITNESSES THERETO.

Robt Holsclaw OF *Little Eagle, SD*
John Littlebear OF *Little Eagle, SD*
Susan Looking Back OF *Little Eagle, SD*

DEPARTMENT OF THE INTERIOR
Office of Indian Affairs
Washington   JAN 25 1921

It is respectfully recommended that the within will of His Horse Looking, Deceased Standing Rock Sioux Allottee No. 397, be approved under the Act of June 25, 1910 (36 Stat. L. 855-6), as amended by the Act of February 14, 1913 (37 Stat. L. 678).

Respectfully,
E. B. Meritt
Assistant Commissioner.

DEPARTMENT OF THE INTERIOR
Office of the Secretary
Washington   FEB -3 1921

The accompanying will of His Horse Looking, deceased Standing Rock Sioux Allottee No. 397, is hereby approved under the Act of June 25, 1910 (36 Stat. L. 855-6), as amended by the Act of February 14, 1913 (37 Stat. L. 678).

SG Hopkins
Assistant Secretary

DEPARTMENT OF THE INTERIOR
Office of the Secretary   MAY 24 1921

It appears from an examination of departmental records subsequent to the above approval that there is a misdescription(sic) of property in the will of His Horse Looking in that the SE 1/4, Sec. 8, T. 20, R. 27, is devised to his grandson Noah Wakuramani instead of the SW 1/4 of said section; that under the provisions of the will he intended to devise his entire estate but in fact made no disposition of the SW 1/4; that clearly he intended to give his said grandson 160 acres of land; and that he did not own the SE 1/4, but did own the SW 1/4. From the foregoing it is to be presumed that testator meant and intended to devise his own land, not the property of another, and as it is obvious that a mistake was made in the description of the land devised to the grandson, the above approval of February 3, 1921, is hereby modified to apply to the will as if it described in this respect the SW 1/4, Sec 8, instead of the SE 1/4, of said section.

F M Goodwin
Assistant Secretary

▲▼▲▼▲▼▲▼▲▼▲▼▲▼

WILLIAM PEREAU

W I L L.

IN THE NAME OF GOD AMEN:

I, William Pereau Fort Pect(sic) allottee No. 1592 residing at Poplar, Montana, being of sound mind but of feeble health and realizing the uncertainty of life, and not acting under fraud, duress, menace or undue influence, do this

10th day of July, 1918, make, publish and declare the following to be my last will and testament.

First:

I give, devise and bequeath to my sister, Regina Pereau, Fort Peck allottee No. ____ a one half interest in the following described lands, S/2 of NW ¼ and Lots 3 4 Sec. 5, T. 32 N., R. 48 E. And the E/2 of NW ¼ of SE/4 Sec. 12, T. 26 N., R. 45 E. And SW/4 of SE/4 Sec. 25, T. 27 N. R. 45 E being my own allotment on the Fort Peck reservation. Also SE/4 & S/2 of NE/4 and Lots 1 & 2 Sec. 1 T. 32 N R. 48 E. and W/2 of SE/4 Sec. 12, T. 26 N., R. 45 E. and NW/4 of SE/4 Sec. 25. T. 27 N., R. 45 E. being the allotment of my dead wife Maggie H. Pereau, Fort Peck Allottee #1749. Also SW/4, W/2SE/4(sic) Sec. 34, T. 33N., R. 49 E. being the allotment of my dead son William H.A. Pereau, Fort Peck allottee #2314.

Second:

I give, devise and bequeath the remaining one half interest in the above described lands to Violet Ivey Pereau, Fort Peck allottee #___.

I also give devise and bequeath, Regina Pereau and to Violet I. Pereau any and all other property of which I may die possessed, share and share alike.

I hereby appoint E.D. Mossman, Supt. of Fort Peck Agency, or his successor in office, as executor of my estate.

(Signed)   **William Pereau**
Fort Peck allottee No. ____

Witness:

Burton F. Roth
Henry Shields

We, the undersigned, hereby certify on our honor that neither of us are related in any way to the testator, that we were both present and witnessed the signature of the testator to the above instrument in one page which he read and fully understood before signing as he was apparently of sound mind and signed the same of his own free will and accord stating that his wishes were duly set forth.   **Burton F. Roth**
Henry Shields

Indian Wills, 1911 – 1921 Book 1
Records of The Bureau of Indian Affairs

No. 442 Filed Oct. 30th 1918 O.R. Girard Clerk of District Court. Recorded in Book of Wills page 58.

STATE OF MONTANA,

COUNTY OF SHERIDAN. } ss.

I, **Albert R. Chapman** Clerk of the District Court of the Twentieth Judicial District of the State of Montana, n and for the County of Sheridan, do hereby certify that the above and foregoing is a full, true and correct copy, and the whole thereof, of an original **Will**, **in the matter of the estate of William Pureau, deceased** now on file in my office.

IN WITNESS WHEREOF, I have hereunto set my hand and affixed the seal of said court this **4th day** of **October** A.D. 1920

Albert Chapman
Clerk of the District Court.

By ....
Deputy Clerk

SCALPER

LAST WILL AND TESTAMENT OF SCALPER,
CROW CREEK ALLOTTEE, NUMBER 803
--------- 0 -------

<u>IN THE NAME OF GOD, AMEN</u>:

I, Scapler, 75 years of age, a member of the Crow Creek reservation in the state of South Dakota, being of sound mind, memory, and understanding, hereby do make and publish this my last will and testament, hereby revoking and annulling all wills by me heretofore made, that is to say:

<u>FIRST</u>:   I direct that all my just debts and funeral expenses and the expenses of my last illness shall be paid as soon after my decease as shall be convenient.

<u>SECOND</u>: I am posessed(sic) of an allotment of land on the Crow Creek reservation, in the state of South Dakota, said allotment being described as the N1/2-23-107-71-W., 5th P.M. South Dakota, same having been allotted to me

under the Act of March 2, 1889 (25 Stat. L. 888), a portion of said land pm the Crow Creek reservation on June 9, 1919, said portion being described as the NW1/4-23-107-71, the remainder of said allotment, I give, devise, and bequeath to the following names persons, to-wit:

To my wife, Red, 71 years of age, the NE1/4-23-1-7-71, W., 5th P.M. South Dakota, containing 160 acres.

The portion of my allotment which was sold was sold for $1665.00, said sale having as yet not been approved by the Department, if the same should be approved I desire to give to my stepson Joseph All Around $500.00. To my cousin Eagle Road, known as Mrs. Fearless Hawk, $200.00, and the balance to go to my wife, Red.

I have a mower and rake, which I give, devise and bequeath to my step-son, Joseph All Around.

My two horses, wagon and harness I give, devise and bequeath to my wife Red, for her to have and do with as she pleases.

I also have a hay rack, which I give, devise and bequeath to Day, an allottee of this reservation, for his kindness to me during my sickness..

All of my other property, both real and personal, which I may be now or hereafter be posessed(sic) of, I give, devise and bequeath to my wife, Red.

AND LASTLY: I am satisfied that the officers of the Department of the Interior of the United States will make proper provision for carrying into effect of this my last will and testament, and therefore I have not appointed an executor to administer my estate.

Sheet 2 to the will of Scalper.

IN WITNESS WHEREOF, I have set my hand and seal to this my last will and testament at the home of Day, located on the Crow Creek reservation, in the state of South Dakota, this 20th day of October, 1919.

His

SCALPER   (thumb print)

Mark

Signed, sealed, published and declared by the said Scalper, in our presence, as and for his last will and testament, and at his request and in his presence and in the presence of each other we have hereunto subscribed our names as attesting withesses(sic) thereto.

Joe Bad Moccasin
Charles McBride
Peter W. Lightfoot
        All of Ft. Thompson, S. D.

Probate
91148-19

DEPARTMENT OF THE INTERIOR
Office of Indian Affairs   JUN 30 1921

It is hereby recommended that the within will of Scalper, deceased Crow Creek Allottee No. 803, be approved in accordance with the Act of June 25, 1910 (36 Stat. L. 855-6), as amended by the Act of February 14, 1913 (37 Stat. L. 678).
        Respectfully,
        E. B. Meritt
        Assistant Commissioner.

DEPARTMENT OF THE INTERIOR
Office of the Secretary   JUL -1 1921

The within will of Scalper, deceased Crow Creek allottee No. 803, is hereby approved in accordance with the Act of June 25, 1910 (36 Stat. L. 855-6), as amended by the Act of February 14, 1913 (37 Stat. L. 678).

        F M Goodwin
        Assistant Secretary

▲▼▲▼▲▼▲▼▲▼▲▼▲▼▲▼

LITTLE SOLDIER

WILL

I, **Little Soldier** of Pine Ridge Agency, South Dakota, Allottee number **899** do hereby make and declare this to be my last will and testament in accordance with Section 2 of the Act of June 25, 1910, (38 stat. 855-858), and Act of

February 14. 1913, (Public No. 381), hereby revoking all former wills made by us:

1.   I hereby direct that, as soon as possible after my decease, that all my debts, funeral and testamentary expenses be paid out of my personal estate.

2.   I give and devise my allotment on the Pine Ridge Reservation, South Dakota, described as follows:

All of Sec. 7, T 37, R 44.

And my share in estate of my mother, Takes The Gun, Pine Ridge allottee No. 6040.

in the following manner:

NW/4 of Sec. 7, T 37, R 44, to my daughter, Sallie Eagle Louse.

SW/4 of Sec. 7, T 37, R 44, to my son, Harry Little Soldier.

NE/4 of Sec. 7, T 37, R 44, to my wife, Good Road.

SE/4 of Sec. 7, T 37, R 44, to my son, James Little Soldier.

My share in estate of my mother, Takes The Gun, to my daughter, Sallie Eagle Louse.

3.   I give and bequeath all of my personal property of whatsoever nature and wheresoever situated unto **my wife, Good Road. (Property consists of 2 mares, wagon, harness, mower and house.**

4.   All the rest of my property, real or personal, now possessed or hereafter acquired, of whatsoever nature and wheresoever situated, I hereby give, devise and bequeath unto **my wife, Good Road.**

In witness whereof I have hereunto set my hand this **3d** day of **August** 1916

his
Little Soldier (thumb print)
mark

The above statement was this **3d** day of **August** 1916 signed and published by **Little Soldier** as **his** last will and testament in the joint presence of the undersigned, the said **Little Soldier** then being of sound and vigorous mind and free from any constraint or compulsion: whereupon we, being without any interest in the matter other than friendship, and being well acquainted with **him** but not members of **his** family, immediately subscribed our names hereto in the presence of each other and of the said testator, for the purpose of attesting the said will, as .... requested us to do. And that I **H. E. Wright** at the testat**or**'s request, have written **his** name in ink, and that **I** affixed **his** thumb-marks.

Post Office Address.

H.E Wright   **Pine Ridge, S. D.**
(Illegible signature)   **Pine Ridge, S. D.**

Pine Ridge, South Dakota
August 3, 1916.

March 7, 1921.

I hereby certify that I have fully inquired into the mental competency of the Indian, signing the above will; the circumstances attending the execution of the will; the influence that may have induced its execution, and the names of those entitled to share in the estate under the law of descent in South Dakota: reasons for the disposition of the property proposed by the will, differing from disposition had the property descended by operation of law.

I respectfully forward this will with the recommendation that it be --- approved.

H. M. Tidwell
Supt. & Spl. Disb. Agent

DEPARTMENT OF THE INTERIOR
Office of Indian Affairs   APR 22 1921

The within will of Little Soldier, deceased Oglala Sioux allottee #899, is hereby recommended for approval under the Act of June 25, 1910 (36 Stat. L. 855-6), as amended by the Act of February 14, 1913 (37 Stat. L. 678), and the Regulations of the Department.

Respectfully,
E. B. Meritt
Assistant Commissioner.

Indian Wills, 1911 – 1921 Book 1
Records of The Bureau of Indian Affairs

DEPARTMENT OF THE INTERIOR
Office of the Secretary   APR 25 1921

The within will of Little Soldier, deceased Oglala Sioux allottee #899, is hereby approved according to the provisions of the Act of June 25, 1910 (36 Stat. L. 855-6), as amended by the Act of February 14, 1913 (37 Stat. L. 678), and the Regulations of the Department.

S G Hopkins
Assistant Secretary

▲▼▲▼▲▼▲▼▲▼▲▼▲▼

YELLOW WOMAN

In the name of God: Amen.

Being of sound mind and realizing the frailities of this life I here by appoint the superintendent of the Rosebud reservation as my executor, abd(sic) that after he shall have paid all my funeral expenses etc:, I leave to my daughter, Mrs. Alice First Hawk of Ft. Pierre, S. D. and Mr. Silas Yellow Woman of Rosebud, one half (1/2) of all that I may be posessed(sic) of, or inherit at the time of my death. That I hereby leave to my daughter Mrs. Pizola the sum of one dollar ($1.00) and Richard Night Chase the sum of ($1.00). That the reason that I am leaving the bulk of my estate to Mrs. Alice First Hawk is that she has at all times looked after me and kept me until this time and I have not wanted for any thing during the time that I have been with her.

(Illegible signature)

her

(thumb print)

Witness to mark.   Yellow Woman.   mark

Frank Red Hawk

his

witness to mark   (thumb print)

(Illegible signature)
Joseph Medicine Bear

We do here by certify on our honor that the within instrument was subscribed to in our presence, and in the presence of each other and that we are in no way interested as benificiarys(sic). Dated this 22 nd day of July 1920.

(Illegible signature)   *her*

witness to mark   Lisa K Red Hawk (thumb print)
(Illegible signature)
Joseph Medicine Bear

DEPARTMENT OF THE INTERIOR
Office of Indian Affairs   APR -8 1921

It is hereby recommended that the within will be approved under the provisions of the Act of June 25, 1910 (36 Stat. L. 855-6), as amended by the Act of February 14, 1913 (37 Stat. L. 678).

E. B. Meritt
Assistant Commissioner.

DEPARTMENT OF THE INTERIOR
Office of the Secretary   APR 15 1921

The within will is hereby approved under the provisions of the Act of June 25, 1910 (36 Stat. L. 855-6), as amended by the Act of February 14, 1913 (37 Stat. L. 678), and the Regulations of the Department.

S G Hopkins
Assistant Secretary

NOTES NO or NOTEZ NO

WILL

OFFICE OF INDIAN AFFAIRS
RECEIVED
OCT 5- 1920
82136

IN THE NAME OF GOD, AMEN: I, **Notes No age 86** an Indian of the Nez Perce Reservation, Idaho, now residing at **Winona** Idaho, being of sound mind and disposing memory, and not acting under duress, menace, fraud, or undue influence, of any person whatsoever do hereby make, publish and declare this my LAST WILL AND TESTAMENT, in the manner following, that is to say:

First: I direct that my body be decently buried with proper regard to my station in life, and the circumstances of my estate.

Second: I direct that my funeral expenses and expenses of my last illness be paid from any funds belonging to my estate, or in the custody of the Superintendent of the Nez Perce Indian Reservation, Lapwai, Idaho.

Third: I will and bequeath to Charley Stephens and Jeanette Stephens, equally, allotment No. 704, being my own allotment.

Fourth: I will and bequeath to Jeanette Stephens, daughter, all the money deposited to my credit at the Nez Perce Agency of which I may die possessed. Also Allotment 680, my 1/3 interest in No. 679, 1/6 of No. 1851, 1/15 of No. 471.

My reasons for giving my daughter, Jeanette Stephens, more than to my son, Charley Stephens, are that Jeanette has always taken care of me, is single and has to support herself, while my son has not taken care of me, and is able bodied and can easily support himself.

In witness whereof, I have hereunto put my hand and seal this **3rd** day pf **September** 1920.
Her

Notes no   (thumb print)
mark

The foregoing instrument was on the date hereof signed, sealed, published and declared by said **Notes no** to be her LAST WILL AND TESTAMENT, in the presence of us, and at her request and in her presence, and in the presence of each other, we have subscribed our names as witnesses on this **3rd** day of **September** 1920

Corbett Lawyer
Rita E Brock
David McFarland

Probate
15251-21

DEPARTMENT OF THE INTERIOR
Office of Indian Affairs   MAY -2 1921
The within will of Notez-no is hereby recommended for approval in accordance with the provisions of the Act of June 25, 1910 (36 Stat. L. 855-6), as amended by the Act of February 14, 1913 (37 Stat. L. 678).

E. B. Meritt
Assistant Commissioner.

DEPARTMENT OF THE INTERIOR
Office of the Secretary   MAY 31 1921
The within will is hereby approved according to the provisions of the Act of June 25, 1910 (36 Stat. L. 855-6), as amended by the Act of February 14, 1913 (37 Stat. L. 678).

F M Goodwin
Assistant Secretary

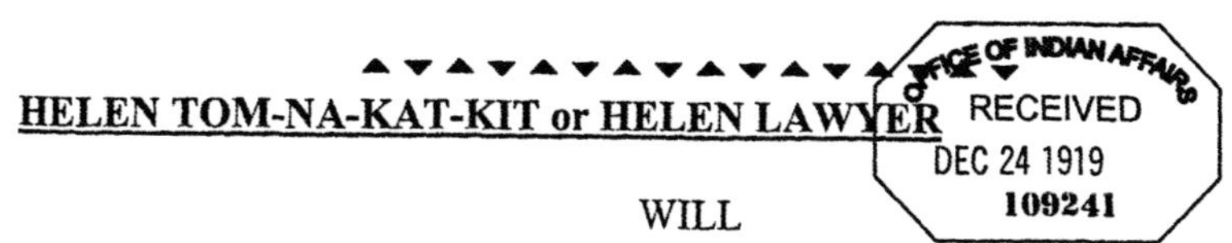

HELEN TOM-NA-KAT-KIT or HELEN LAWYER

WILL

IN THE NAME OF GOD, AMEN I **Helen Tom-na-kat-kit age 78,** an Indian of the Nez Perce Indian Reservation, Idaho, now in disposing memory, and not acting under duress, menace, fraud, or undue influence, of any person whatsoever, do hereby make, publish and declare this my LAST WILL AND TESTAMENT, in the manner following, that is to say:

First: I direct that my body be decently buried with the proper regard to my station in life, and the circumstances of my estate.

Second: I direct that my funeral expenses and expenses of my last illness be paid from any funds belonging to my estate, or in the custody of the Superintendent of the Nez Perce Indian Reservation, Lapwai, Idaho.

Third: I will and bequeath to Peter Slickpoo, half-brother, my allotment, No. 780, described as lots 3, 4, 13 & 14, Section 33, Township 34 N. Range 2 W. B. M., 80 acres.

Jim Slickpoo and Paul Slickpoo, half-brothers, and Nema Lawyer, sister, my other legal heirs, I disinherit for the reason that they have their own allotments and inherited interests, while Peter Slickpoo does not have as much as the others and has always looked after me and cared for my interests.

I have no other interests nor any personal property.

In witness whereof, I have hereunto put my hand and seal this **10th** day of **Nov 1919.**

Her
Helen Tomnakatkit (thumb print)
Mark

The foregoing instrument was on the date hereof signed, sealed, published and declared by said **Helen Tom-na-kat-kit** to be her LAST WILL AND TESTAMENT, in the presence of us, and at her request and in her presence, and in the presence of each other, we have subscribed our names as witnesses on this **10** day of **November 1919**

> *Chett B. Sawyer*
> (Illegible signature)
> (Illegible signature)

Probate
109241-19
 37915-21
  J W H

DEPARTMENT OF THE INTERIOR
Office of Indian Affairs   MAY 27 1921

The within will of Helen Lawyer, (Tom-na-kat-kit), deceased Nez Perce allottee #780, is hereby recommended for approval under the Act of June 25, 1910 (36 Stat. L. 855-6), as amended by the Act of February 14, 1913 (37 Stat. L. 678).

> *E. B. Meritt*
> Assistant Commissioner.

DEPARTMENT OF THE INTERIOR
Office of the Secretary   JUN -8 1921

The within will of Helen Lawyer, (Tom-na-kat-kit), deceased Nez Perce allottee #780, is hereby approved under the Act of June 25, 1910 (36 Stat. L. 855-6), as amended by the Act of February 14, 1913 (37 Stat. L. 678), and the Regulations of the Department.

> *F M Goodwin*
> Assistant Secretary

ROSEBUD AGENCY, S.D.
RECEIVED
SEP (?) 1921
FILE ______________

ALEXANDER (ALEX) LARVIE

Will of Alexander Larvie.

I, Alexander Larvie also known as Alex Larvie, a resident of Mellette County, South Dakota, whose potoffice address is Farley, South Dakota, being of sound mind and memory, and considering the uncertainty of life, do hereby make, publish, ordain and declare this to be my last will and testament.

FIRST: I order and direct that my executor hereinafter named, pay all my just debts and funeral expenses as soon after my decease as conveniently may be.

SECOND: After the payment of such debts and funeral expenses I give, devise and bequeath to my children, Julia Flood, Louisa Wright, Benjamin Larvie, Rose Breast, Helen Gerry, Peter Larvie, Albert Larvie, Alexander Larvie and Melissa Larvie, each, two mares and one cow; to be selected from my herds by my executor hereinafter named and given to said children respectfully; and I hereby give, devise and bequeath all the remaining personal property of which I may die possessed to my wife, Molly Larvie.

THIRD: I hereby give, devise and bequeath to my wife, Molly Larvie, one-third of any and all interest in real property of which I may die seized and possessed, the remainder and residue of all real property to be divided equally amoung my children; Julia Flood, Louisa Wright, Benjamin Larvie, Rose Breast, Helen Gerry, Peter Larvie, Albert Larvie, Alexander Larvie, and Melissa Larvie.

FOURTH: I hereby make, constitute and appoint O. A. Hodson an officer of the Belvidere State Bank, -residing at Belvidere, South Dakota, to be the executor of this my last will and testament hereby revoking all former wills by me made.

IN TESTIMONY WHEREOF, I have hereunto subscribed my name and affixed my seal this 18th day of June, 1917.

His
Alexander Larvie X
mark

Witness to mark:

R. Guenard.
Glenn W. Martins.

I hereby certify that I have examined the foregoing copy in detail and find it to correspond with the original.

(Illegible signature)
Notary Public

DEPARTMENT OF THE INTERIOR
Office of Indian Affairs

Indian Wills, 1911 – 1921 Book 1
Records of The Bureau of Indian Affairs

The within will is hereby recommended for approval under the provisions of the Act of June 25, 1910 (36 Stat. L. 855-6), as amended by the Act of February 14, 1913 (37 Stat. L. 678).

E. B. Meritt
Assistant Commissioner.

DEPARTMENT OF THE INTERIOR
Office of the Secretary   JUN -8 1921

The within will is hereby approved under the provisions of the Act of June 25, 1910 (36 Stat. L. 855-6), as amended by the Act of February 14, 1913 (37 Stat. L. 678), and the Regulations of the Department.

F M Goodwin
Assistant Secretary

▲▼▲▼▲▼▲▼▲▼▲▼▲▼▲▼

<u>HARRY HUNTS ALONG or THUNDER HAWK</u>

Elbowoods N. Dak.
Feb 23ᵈ 1918

E. W. Jermark Supt. --
Elbowoods, N. Dak.   *Exhibit A*

Sir, ---

This morning I make a will to my mother Sarah Hunts Along and my brother John Hunts Along. They will divid(sic) up all my land and all my money. I don't want to let my father have any of my land or money. I have been trying to make a will to my mother and brother long ago but this morning it comes sudden that one of my sores on my side open up came the blood.

This is my own hand writing.

Harry Hunts Along
Elbowoods

Toney Birds Bill
C. R. Sylvester
Roger Brown

Probate
35703-21
JMP

DEPARTMENT OF THE INTERIOR
Office of Indian Affairs   JUN -8 1921

The within will of Thunder Hawk or Harry Hunts Along, deceased allottee Nos. 181, 1589 and 543a of the Fort Berthold Reservation, North Dakota is hereby recommended for approval under the Act of June 25, 1910 (36 Stat. L. 855-6), as amended by the Act of February 14, 1913 (37 Stat. L. 678).

> Respectfully,
> *E. B. Meritt*
> Assistant Commissioner.

DEPARTMENT OF THE INTERIOR
Office of the Secretary   JUN -8 1921

The within will of Thunder Hawk or Harry Hunts Along, deceased allottee Nos. 181, 1589 and 543a of the Fort Berthold Reservation, North Dakota is hereby approved in accordance with the Act of June 25, 1910 (36 Stat. L. 855-6), as amended by the Act of February 14, 1913 (37 Stat. L. 678).

> *F M Goodwin*
> Assistant Secretary

▲▼▲▼▲▼▲▼▲▼▲▼▲▼

GEORGE WILLIAMS

IN THE NAME OF GOD, AMEN. I, George Williams of the county of Mineral, state of Nevada, of the age of 57, and being of sound and disposing mind and memory, and not acting under duress, menance(sic), fraud, or undue influence of any person whatever, do make, publish and declare this my last will and testament, in manner following, that is to say:

First. I hereby devise and bequeath unto my good friend Singing McMaster and Tom Benton one half interest each, of that estate know as Mary Williams allotment which is No. 271 and is described as follows W1/2 SE1/4 SW1/4. Sec. 18, T. 19 R. 29 containing twenty acres more or less, which may come to me by inheritance under the decision of the Department of the Interior.

Second: I hereby devise and bequeath unto Annie Nobe, five acres and to Frank Dick, five acres, out and from my allotment No. 53 which is the S1/2 NW·1/4 NE1/4 Sec. 22, T. 13 N. R. 28 E. M. D. B. & M. contain more or less twenty acres. The balance of this allotment ten acres I hereby devise and bequeath unto my wife Mattie Williams, and upon her death the said land hereby bequeathed to her shall become the property of George Kennearim, for him and his heirs forever.

I hereby nominate and appoint the Superintendent of the Walker River Indian Reservation as my executor of this my last will and testament.

In witness whereof I have hereunto set my and and seal this twenty eight day of March, in the year of our Lord, one thousand nine hundred and fourteen.

                                        Thumb mark of George Williams.

Witnesses to mark.
Name   Occupation   Residence   (thumb print)
RC Lyer   Merchant   Schurg, Nev
HV Harbrace   Supt Schu of Nev.

▲▼▲▼▲▼▲▼▲▼▲▼▲▼▲▼

NE-TA-WA-SI-NO-KWE or LIZZIE CATFISH

I, Ne-ta-wa-si-no-kwe (Lizzie Catfish), of Lac du Flambeau in the County of Vilas, in the State of Wisconsin, being of sound mind and memory, do make, publish, and declare this my last will and testament, hereby revoking all other wills, bequests and devices by me made.

First:- I bequeath unto my beloved daughter, Kweans (Rosy Skye) all of my real estate which is described as follows: Lot 3 of SW1/4 of Section 8, Township 40, Range 6E and Lot 1 of NE1/4 of Section 1, Township 41, Range 5 E containing 94.80 acres and I also bequeath to my said daughter the house owned by me situated on the allotment of Chicog, Sr.

Second:- I further bequeath to my said daughter all the personal property and money of which I am possessed at the time of my demise. It is my further wish that my said daughter, Kwe-ans (Rosy Skye), who is a minor, shall be kept and remain in school during her minority.

I do hereby appoint and constitute my father, We-gi-ma-we-jo to act as executor of this my last will and testament after my death.

Indian Wills, 1911 – 1921 Book 1
Records of The Bureau of Indian Affairs

IN WITNESS WHEREOF I have hereunto set my hand and seal this *20th day of December* A.D. 1917.

Witnesses: *Her mark*
WH Shawnee Clerk   *Ne-ta-wa-si-no-kwe (Lizzie Catfish)*
Paul Negamgyz Interpreter   (thumb print)
        Lac du Flambeau, Wis.

The foregoing instrument was signed, sealed, published and declared by the said Ne-ta-wa-si-no-kew (Lizzie Catfish) as and for her last will and testament, in the presence of us, who, at her request, in her presence, and in the presence of each other, have hereunto subscribed our names as attesting witnesses; and said testator was then of sound and disposing mind and memory.

        W H Shawnee
              Clerk
Witnesses:
        Lac du Flambeau, Wis.
    Paul Negamgyz Interpreter
        Lac du Flambeau, Wis.

DEPARTMENT OF THE INTERIOR
WASHINGTON

ADDRESS ONLY
THE SECRETARY OF THE INTERIOR

My dear Mr. President:

There is submitted for your consideration the last will and testament of Ne-ta-wa-si-no-kwe, Chippewa allottee #200 of the Lac da Flambeau Reservation, by which she devises her estate to her daughter, Kweans or Rosy Skye.

The circumstances of the case are found to justify the making of the will and its approval is recommended.

The matter is brought to your attention because by the terms of the allottee's patent, issued under Treaty of September 30, 1854 (10 Stat. L., 1109) the land is restricted against alienation or incumerance during the pleasure of the President of the United States.

Sincerely,
EB Finney
Acting Secretary

The President

The White House

DEPARTMENT OF THE INTERIOR
Office of Indian Affairs

It is respectfully recommended that the within will of Ne-ta-wa-si-no-kwe, be laid before the President for the approval.

Chuck Burber
Commissioner

DEPARTMENT OF THE INTERIOR
Office of the Secretary   MAY 5 1921

It is respectfully recommended that the within will of Ne-ta-wa-si-no-kwe, be approved.

EB Finney
Acting Secretary

THE WHITE HOUSE
May 5, 1921
APPROVED: *Warren G Harding*

▲▼▲▼▲▼▲▼▲▼▲▼▲▼▲▼

HORACE LONG BEAR

1279-18 Crow 353

Last Will and Testament
of
Horace Long Bear

IN THE NAME OF GOD, AMEN:

I, *Horace Long Bear* of *Crow Agency Mont.* being of sound mind, memory, and understanding, do hereby make and publish this my last will and testament, hereby revoking and annulling all wills by me heretofore made, in manner of form following, that is to say:

First; I direct that all my just debts and future expenses, and expenses of my last illness shall be paid by my executor hereinafter named as soon after my decease as convenient;

Second; I give, devise and bequeath to *my wife, Bears that Passes and my mother Fox Goes Out, in equal shares the agricultural portion of my own allotment; to Bears that Passes, Fox Goes Out, Sebastion Long Bear and Knows the Ground in equal shares the agricultural portion of my inherited land. - to Bears that Passes, Fox Goes Out, Sebastion Long Bear, Knows the Ground and Bull Weasel in equal shares the grazing portion of my inherited land. To my wife Bears that Passes one gray mare and colt, harness, mowing machine and any funds under the jurisdiction of the Supt of Crow Agency; to Fox Goes Out one gray team and heavy harness.*

Third; All the rest and residue of my estate, both real and personal and mixed, I give, devise and bequeath to my lawful heirs as determined after my decease.

And lastly: I do hereby nominate, constitute and appoint *Supt Crow Agency* executor of this my last will and testament.

In testimony Whereof, I have set my hand and seal to this, my last will and Testament at *Crow Agency* Montana, this *2d* day of *April* in the year of our Lord one thousand nine hundred and *fifteen.*

Horace Long Bear

Signed, sealed, published and declared by said *Horace Long Bear* in our presence, as and for *his* last Will and testament, and at *his* request and in our presence, and in the presence of each other, we have hereunto subscribed our names as attesting witnesses thereto.

Christine C. Burns	of	*Crow Agency*
Josephine Laforge	of	*Crow Agency*
C D Munro	of	*Crow Agency Mont*

Probate
1279-18
RTB

DEPARTMENT OF THE INTERIOR
Office of Indian Affairs   MAY 25 1921

It is hereby recommended that the within will of Horace Long Bear, Crow allottee No. 560, be approved in accordance with the Act of June 25, 1910 (36 Stat. L. 855-6), as amended by the Act of February 14, 1913 (37 Stat. L. 678). No executor will be recognized.

> Respectfully,
> *E. B. Meritt*
> Assistant Commissioner.

DEPARTMENT OF THE INTERIOR
Office of the Secretary   JUN 10 1921

The within will of Horace Long Bear, Crow allottee NO. 560, is hereby approved in accordance with the Act of June 25, 1910 (36 Stat. L. 855-6), as amended by the Act of February 14, 1913 (37 Stat. L. 678). No executor will be recognized.

> *F M Goodwin*
> Assistant Secretary

▲▼▲▼▲▼▲▼▲▼▲▼▲▼▲▼

<u>OWNS THE MULE</u>

LAST WILL AND TESTAMENT.

IN THE NAME OF GOD, AMEN, I, *Owns the Mule* of the Cheyenne River Reservation, in the County of *Ziebach* and State of South Dakota, being of sound mind and memory, and considering the uncertainty of this frail and transitory life, do therefore make, ordain, publish and declare this to be my last Will and Testament.

FIRST, I order and direct that my Execut*or* hereinafter names, pay all my just debts and funeral expenses as soon after my decease as conveniently may he.

SECOND: After the payment of such funeral expenses and debts, I give, devise, and bequeath:- *unto Moses Straight Head, my nephew, all my property consisting of One Section (640 acres) land that I inherit from my husband Fat*

Fox and my allotment, consisting of 320 acres and all my allotment benefits as inherited from my husband and my own.

Fat Fox Allotment, inherited SE4 of Sec. 18, T. 14 N & S2 Sec. 21, SE4 of Sec. 20, T. 13 N., R. 20 E of B.H.M. My own allotment described as NE4, E2 of NW4 and Lots 1 & 2 of Sec. 19, T. 14 N., R. 20 E. Black Hills Meridian.

Lastly, I make, constitute and appoint, *F.C. Campbell, Supt.*, as my Execut*or* to serve without bond to be Execut*or* of this Last Will and Testament, hereby revolking(sic) all former Wills by me made.

IN TESTIMONY WHEREOF, I have hereunto subscribed my name and affixed my seal, the *22nd* day of *June* in the year of our Lord one Thousand Nine Hundred *Fifteen*.

Witnesses

Forrest R Stone   *her*
                                            Owns The Mule (thumb print)
Robert Yellow Breast   mark

This instrument was on the day and the date thereof, signed, published and declared by said testator *Owns the Mule* to be Las(sic) Will and Testament, in our presence, who, at his request, have subscribed our names hereunto, as witnesses, in his presence, and in the presence of each other.

Forrest R Stone   Residing at   *Dupree S.D.*
Robert Yellow Breast   Residing at   *Dupree So Dak*

DEPARTMENT OF THE INTERIOR
Office of Indian Affairs   DEC 27 1920

It is hereby recommended that the within will of Owns the Mule, deceased Cheyenne River Sioux allottee No. 2087, be approved according to the provisions of the Act of June 25, 1910 (36 Stat. L. 855-6), as amended by the Act of February 14, 1913 (37 Stat. L. 678).

Respectfully,
E. B. Meritt
Assistant Commissioner.

DEPARTMENT OF THE INTERIOR
Office of the Secretary   DEC 29 1920

The within will of Owns the Mule, deceased Cheyenne River Sioux allottee No. 2087, is hereby approved according to the provisions of the Act of June 25, 1910 (36 Stat. L. 855-6), as amended by the Act of February 14, 1913 (37 Stat. L. 678).

S G Hopkins
Assistant Secretary

▲▼▲▼▲▼▲▼▲▼▲▼▲▼▲▼

<u>FRED JOHNSON</u>

LAST WILL AND TESTAMENT

I, Fred Johnson, of sound mind and memory, realizing the uncertaintity(sic) of life, do execute and establish this my last will and testament, revoking all former wills by me made.

I hereby request and direct that all my just debts and my funeral expenses be paid as soon as may be after my death.

My allotment, described as the SW/4 of Sec. 36 in Twp 34 S of R 8 E of the Willamette meridian in Oregon, I devise and bequeath in equal shares to my sister Sedonia Johnson and to my cousin Bertha Beal George. This bequest is in token of my love and affection for my sister Sedonia, and in grateful acknowledgement of the care and assistance given me by my cousin Bertha Beal George during my present illness.

To my father, Edward A. Johnson, to my half-sister, Hazel Wilson, and to my half-brother, Marshall Coney, I bequeath to each one dollar. Also one dollars each to my half-brothers Edward Vernie and Rowley Johnson.

I am unmarried, and without issue, and know of no other possible claimants to my property other than those mentioned above, and it is my desire that my property descend to my sister Sedonia and to my cousin Bertha George, (or to their heirs), both real and personal, in equal shares to the said Sedonia Johnson and Bertha George.

Fred Johnson

We, the undersigned, hereby certify that we have witnessed the signing of the foregoing instrument by Fred Johnson who declared that the same represented his wishes and that he understood the meaning of the instrument. We further certify that we have affixed our signatures at the request and in the presence of Fred Johnson, whom we believe to be of sound mind and memory.

H B Jolley

Klamath Agency, Ore.,
    Mar. 31, 1920.   *C Edward Dennis*

DEPARTMENT OF THE INTERIOR
Office of Indian Affairs   DEC 23 1920

The within will of Fred Johnson, deceased allottee No. 716 of the Klamath Tribe, is respectfully recommended for approval pursuant to the provisions of the Act of June 25, 1910 (36 Stat. L. 855-6), as amended by the Act of February 14, 1913 (37 Stat. L. 678).

Respectfully,
C F Hawke
Acting Assistant Commissioner.

DEPARTMENT OF THE INTERIOR
Office of the Secretary   DEC 28 1920

The within will of Fred Johnson, deceased allottee No. 716 of the Klamath Tribe is hereby approved pursuant to the provisions of the Act of June 25, 1910 (36 Stat. L. 855-6), as amended by the Act of February 14, 1913 (37 Stat. L. 678).

S G Hopkins
Assistant Secretary

▲▼▲▼▲▼▲▼▲▼▲▼▲▼▲▼

ELIZABETH CADOTTE

Wakpala, SD
Jan. 13, 1917

I, Elizabeth Cadotte, of Wakpala   County of Corson, State of South Dakota, being of sound mind and memory, do make, publish and declare this to be my last will and testament, to wit:-

1ˢᵗ All my just debts and funeral expenses shall be first fully paid.

2<u>nd</u> I give, devise and bequeath to my son, Gilbert Cadotte the following:

The NE1/4 of Sec. 27- 20- 29, 160 acres, being half of my original allotment. I am fully aware that the land is being held in trust by the United States government but never the less, this is my wish. Also to my son, Gilbert Cadotte, I give, 1 gelding, 6 yrs old, branded 850 on r(sic) th(sic) called Browny.

To my daughter, Mary Louise Cadotte, I give the NW1/4 of Sc. 27- 20- 29 E B.H.M. and this house and all of its contents and the irrigated ground to stand on, also 1 gray mare, 9 yrs old, branded 850 r. th.

My share of my husbands(sic) allotment shall be divided equally among my children; John Cadotte, Benj. Cadotte, Susan Hochner, Mary Louise Cadotte, and Gilbert Cadotte.

I give, devise and bequeath all of the above mentioned property both real and personal as herein stated to my heirs as above mentioned.

To have to hold to them my said children, and to their heirs and assigns forever.

In giving my allotment to only two of my children, namely Gilbert and Mary Louise, I have this to say, I want my allotment to be held forever by these two of my children but it is agreed between these and myself that their allotments shall be exchanged with mine and their allotments shall be probated as tho(sic) it was my original allotment and the other children herein named some other part of my will shall get their share, share and share alike. I heir 80 acres from husband allotment which the house stands on that shall go to Mary Louise as stated before.

I nominate and appoint Mr. Claude C. Coxey, Supt. Standing Rock sch(sic) - Ft Yates, N Dak. to be the executor of this my last will and testament, hereby revoking all former wills by me made.

In witness where of I have hereunto set my hand and seal this 13th day of January, A.D. 1917.   her
                                        Elizabeth Cadotte

                                        mark

Signed, sealed, published and declared as and for her last will and testament by the above named testator, in our presence, who have at her request and in her presence, and in the presence of each other, signed our names as witnesses thereto.

Sam Lapointe Farmer
Luke Two Hearts

DEPARTMENT OF THE INTERIOR
Office of Indian Affairs

It is respectfully recommended that the within will of Elizabeth Cadotte be approved under the Act of June 25, 1910 (36 Stat. L. 855-6), as amended by the Act of February 14, 1913 (37 Stat. L. 678).

E B Meritt
Assistant Commissioner

DEPARTMENT OF THE INTERIOR
Office of the Secretary

The within will of Elizabeth Cadotte is hereby approved under the Act of June 25, 1910 (36 Stat. L. 855-6), as amended by the Act of February 14, 1913 (37 Stat. L. 678).

S G Hopkins
Assistant Secretary

▲▼▲▼▲▼▲▼▲▼▲▼▲▼▲▼

NELSON SUCATUMCH

LAST WILL AND TESTAMENT OF NELSON SACATUMCH,

KLAMATH ALLOTTEE NO. 1408
Klamath School, Oregon.

I, Nelson Sucatumch, Klamath Allottee No. 1408, of the Klamath Reservation, County of Klamath and State of Oregon, aged about 100 years, being of sound mind and memory, do hereby make, publish and declare this to be my last will and testament, in manner and form as follows:-

First:-   It is my will that the expenses of my last illness and my funeral expenses be paid, and such debts as may lawfully be paid under the laws of the United States and the regulations promulgated thereunder.

Secondly:- I give, devise and bequeath unto Polly Miller, my niece, who has cared for me for many years, to have and to hold unto the said Polly Miller, her heirs and assigns forever, Lot 8 of Section 4, Township Thirty-five (35), Range Seven (7) East of the Willamette Meridian, Oregon, containing *17.20* acres.

Thirdly:-   I give, devise and bequeath all the rest and residue of my estate unto my son, John Nelson, aged **70** years, of whatsoever kind the said property may be, whether real, personal or mixed, or wheresoever located, to have and to hold unto the said John Nelson, his heirs and assigns, forever. The residue of my estate consists of my allotment on the Klamath Reservation, in Oregon excepting the devise made above to Polly Miller, being particularly described as follows:-

The Lots 10 and 11, the S/2 or the NE/4 of the SE/4, and the S/2 of the N/2 of the NE/4 of the SE/4 of Sec. 22; and the S/2 of the NW/4 of the NW/4, and the S/2 of the N/2 of the NW/4 of the SW/4 of Sec. 23, in Twp. 34 S. and the Lot 7, of Sec. 4, in Twp. 35 S., all in Range 7 East of the Willamette Meridian, Oregon, containing 157.84 acres (less the acreage of Lot 8, Section 4, devised above to Polly Miller). Trust patent issued July 26, 1915.

together with certain funds held in trust by me by the government of the United States; under the Superintendent of the Klamath Indian School, Klamath Agency, Oregon.

Fourthly. I hereby revoke any and allformer(sic) wills by me made.

Fifthly. I nominate and appoint the Superintendent of the Klamath Indian School, Klamath Agency, Oregon, whoever he may be at the time of my death, Executor of this my last will and testament.

In witness whereof I have hereunto set my hand and seal and published and declared this my last will and testament, this 2nd day of July, 1918, at Chiloquin, Oregon.   Her

                                                                                        Right

                                Nelson Sucatumch

                                                                                        Thumb Mark.

The foregoing instrument, consisting of one page besides this, was, by the said Nelson Sucatumch, signed, sealed, published and declared by her to be her last will and testament, in our presence, and we, at her request, and in her presence, and in the presence of each other, have hereunto signed our names as subscribing witnesses this 2nd day of July, 1918, at Chiloquin, Oregon.

Fred A. Baker	residing at Klamath Agency, Oregon.
Rose Wright	residing at Klamath Agency, Oregon.
R W Dawini Hart	residing at Chiloquin, Oregon.

Probate
94596-20
 J W H

DEPARTMENT OF THE INTERIOR
Office of Indian Affairs   DEC 23 1920

The within will of Nelson Sucatumch, deceased allottee No. 1408 of the Klamath Tribe, is respectfully recommended for approval pursuant to the provisions of the Act of June 25, 1910 (36 Stat. L. 855-6), as amended by the Act of February 14, 1913 (37 Stat. L. 678).

> Respectfully,
> *E. B. Meritt*
> Assistant Commissioner.

DEPARTMENT OF THE INTERIOR
Office of the Secretary   DEC 29 1920

The within will of Nelson Sucatumch, deceased allottee No. 1408 of the Klamath Tribe is hereby approved pursuant to the provisions of the Act of June 25, 1910 (36 Stat. L. 855-6), as amended by the Act of February 14, 1913 (37 Stat. L. 678).

> *S G Hopkins*
> Assistant Secretary

▲▼▲▼▲▼▲▼▲▼▲▼▲▼▲▼

<u>CHARLEY HAWK</u>

Last Will and Testament

Indian Wills, 1911 – 1921 Book 1
Records of The Bureau of Indian Affairs

I, Charley Hawk, do make my will as follows 3/4 Section of my land to Mrs. Lillie Hawk my wife and 1/2 section of land to Isaac Hawk my son, all the above estate I devise and bequeath as stated for their use and full benefit.

Witness	*F Godfrey*		*his*
to	*Wakpala, S.D.*	*Charley Hawk*	
Mark	*Mrs. F Godfrey*		*mark*
	Wakpala, S.D.		

Dated Feb 26, 1919

Subscribed, sealed and declared by Charley Hawk, Testator, aboved(sic) named as and for his last will in presence of each of us who at his request in his presence in the presence of each other at the same time have hereunto subscribed our names as witnesses this 26th day of February at Wakpala, S.D.

Mrs. F. Godfrey

John Whitesell

Comm Exp Jan 17-1922
Floss Godfrey
Notary Public Corson Co, S.D.

Probate
84732--20

DEPARTMENT OF THE INTERIOR
United States Indian Service
Washington

NOV 30 1920

It is respectfully recommended that the within will of Charley Hawk be approved under the Act of June 25, 1910 (36 Stat. L. 855-6), as amended by the Act of February 14, 1913 (37 Stat. L. 678).

Respectfully,
E B Meritt
Assistant Commissioner

DEPARTMENT OF THE INTERIOR
Office of the Secretary
Washington

DEC -7 1920

The within will of Charley Hawk is hereby approved under the Act of June 25, 1910 (36 Stat. L. 855-6), as amended by the Act of February 14, 1913 (37 Stat. L. 678).

S G Hopkins
Assistant Secretary

▲▼▲▼▲▼▲▼▲▼▲▼▲▼▲▼

ADAM WHITEEAGLE

LAST WILL AND TESTAMENT

Adam Whiteeagle, Standing Rock Indian Allottee No. 528,

IN THE NAME OF GOD, AMEN.

I, **Adam Whiteeagle** OF **Fort Yates, N. D.,** BEING OF SOUND MIND, MEMORY AND UNDERSTANDING, DO HEREBY MAKE AND PUBLISH THIS MY LAST WILL AND TESTAMENT, HEREBY REVOKING AND ANNULLING ALL WILLS BY ME HERETOFORE MADE, IN MANNER AND FORM FOLLOWING. THAT IS TO SAY.

FIRST; I DIRECT THAT ALL MY JUST DEBTS AND FUNERAL(sic) EXPENSES, AND EXPENSES OF MY LAST ILLNESS SHALL BE PAID BY MY EXECUTOR HEREINAFTER NAMED AS SOON AFTER M DECEASE AS CONVENIENT;

SECOND; I GIVE, DEVISE AND BEQUEATH TO **following persons:**

Mrs. Adam Whiteeagle, or Tacanonpawambli, my wife, the SE/4, Sec. 6, Twp. 19 N, R. 28 E, B.H.M., containing 160.00 acres, in South Dakota;

Benjiman(sic) White, my nephew, the S/2 of NE/4, lots 1 and 2; and SE/4 of NW/4, and lots 3, 4 and 5, Sec. 6, Twp. 19 N., R. 28 E., B.H.M., containing 313.06 acres in South Dakota;

Mrs. Abie White, wife of my nephew (Benjamin White), the E/2 of SW/4 and lots 6 and 7, Sec. 6, Twp. 19 N., R. 28 E., B.H.M., containing 152.64 acres in South Dakota.

The above devised land is allotted to me on the Standing Rock Indian Reservation under serial number 528, and represents my original allotment.

THIRD;   ALL THE REST AND RESIDUE OF MY ESTATE BOTH REAL, AND PERSONAL AND MIXED, I GIVE, DEVISE AND BEQUEATH TO MY LAWFUL HEIRS AS DETERMINED AFTER MY DECEASE.

AND, I DO HEREBY NOMINATE, CONSTITURE AND APPOINT   ##############
EXECUTOR OF THIS MY LAST WILL AND TESTAMENT.

IN TESTIMONY, WHEREOF, I HAVE SET MY HAND AND SEAL TO THIS, MY LAST WILL AND TESTAMENT, AT **Fort Yates, North Dakota** THIS *15th* DAY OF **January** IN THE YEAR OF OUR LORD ONE THOUSAND, NINE HUNDRED AND **seventeen**.

AND LASTLY, I HEREBY REQUEST **Asa Littlecrow** TO SIGN MY NAME TO THIS MY LAST WILL AND TESTAMENT AND WITNESS THE SAME.

His

Adam Whiteeagle
TESTATOR OR TESTATRIX   *mark*

SIGNED, SEAL**ed**, PUBLISH**ed** AND DECLARED BY SAID **Adam Whiteeagle**, IN OUR PRESENCE AND FOR **his** LAST WILL AND TESTAMENT.   AND AT **his** REQUEST AND IN OUR PRESENCE, AND IN THE PRESENCE OF EACH OTHER, WE HAVE HEREUNTO SUBSCRIBED OUR NAMES AS ATTESTING WITNESSES THERETO.

Asa Finberger	OF	**Fort Yates, N. D.**
Thomas Frosted	OF	**Fort Yates, N. D.**
Thomas Kidder	OF	**Fort Yates, N. D.**

DEPARTMENT OF THE INTERIOR
United States Indian Service
Washington

It is respectfully recommended that the within will of Adam White Eagle be approved under the Act of June 25, 1910 (36 Stat. L. 855-6), as amended by the Act of February 14, 1913 (37 Stat. L. 678).

C F Hawke
Acting Assistant Commissioner

DEPARTMENT OF THE INTERIOR
Office of the Secretary
Washington   JAN -3 1921

Indian Wills, 1911 – 1921 Book 1
Records of The Bureau of Indian Affairs

The accompanying will of Adam White Eagle is hereby approved under the Act of June 25, 1910 (36 Stat. L. 855-6), as amended by the Act of February 14, 1913 (37 Stat. L. 678).

S G Hopkins
Assistant Secretary

▲▼▲▼▲▼▲▼▲▼▲▼▲▼▲▼